JESUS
IS EVERYTHING

Discovering It All When There's Nothing Left but Jesus

I0143308

DR. BRUCE L. HARTMAN

HIGH BRIDGE BOOKS
HOUSTON

Contents

Prologue

When Nothing Is Left but Jesus

Through Him all things were made; without Him
nothing was made that has been made.

—John 1:3

An elderly man resolutely allowed his son

and a hospice nurse to help him into a hospital bed. A few days earlier, the bed was delivered and placed in his home's living room. He knew the bed would be the beginning of the end of his life.

For two days, unable to move very far, he had sat solemnly looking at the bed, knowing this would be his last place of rest before he departed this earth. His reluctance wasn't nervousness. He had needed to think about things before moving to the bed.

Always thoughtful and diligent, he mentally worked through the meaning of this next step. Like most things in his life, he had to think things out and be sure of what he was doing. Whenever he spoke, which wasn't often, he carefully chose his words. Most of his actions were well thought out. And so would be this final step.

Days earlier, in a progressively weakened state, he had fallen and had to be carried into his home. Embarrassed, he sat on his couch in his familiar spot. Now, unable to move, he had found a temporary place to be. His wife had called his doctor, who was aware of his declining state. The doctor told his family, *The end is near. You need to call in-home hospice. They will help you provide him comfort.* There was no illness. The effects of aging had brought him to the brink.

No longer did the news matter to the man. Nor did his money or even a simple act like shaving. Everything had been eliminated as necessary except for this state of transition. His final decision to move to the hospice bed was encouraged by a nurse who told him this would be a better place to be while waiting for the inevitable. He went to the bed.

His family quickly gathered to help and say goodbye. Each of his children and grandchildren, eighteen souls, spoke with him through tears. They all told him they loved him. In turn, he said to each one, *I love you, too.* It was a wonderful gift that each grandchild, his children, and his wife received before he departed.

As the next few days passed, he became weaker, drifting in and out of consciousness. He heard words of love and exhortations that he was going home to be with Jesus.

On his final day, gentle music played, and his family was near. Most of the day, he was asleep. In his last moments, the man was read a poem by his son.

"I Hope You Know"

I hope you know how much you're loved.
I hope you know how many lives you've touched.
I hope you know how much we care.
I hope you know Jesus is waiting for you.

I know when you cross over the bridge, you will
    find peace.
I know Jesus has a place for you.

I know you will find rest.

I know you will be safe.

Moments after he heard the poem, he opened his eyes, looked at his wife, and said, *I love you.* And then he was gone.

At the end of his life here on earth, everything had become meaningless except for his family and Jesus. Gone were the days when he was a great executive. He no longer needed his clothes or food. He was left only with love and knowing Jesus was waiting for him. Just love and Jesus were important in his final moments here on earth.

We can view this story as bittersweet, and it is. Bitter for the loss of a loved one. Sweet because the family and the man knew Jesus was waiting for him. This event reminds me of Billy Graham, who said, *My home is in heaven. I'm just traveling through this world.* For the man, this truth became confirmed in his final few moments.

When Jesus held his hand in those last minutes, he knew everything he had heard about Jesus was true. When everything was gone, and he was left with only Jesus, he found the permanency of Jesus. In his final moments, Jesus had become everything.

Choosing Jesus

A simple question can be asked for those of us not on the brink between heaven and earth. Do we make Jesus everything and the central figure of our lives, or do we continue to float down the river of life the world offers?

The ultimate reality is always that we can only choose from the choices we have. The man in his final moments was left with one option: accept that Jesus was waiting for him.

For those of us remaining behind, Jesus is the option we can make today. Choosing Jesus is made difficult because swirling around us every minute is temptation and the ways of the world. Not just obvious temptations but also the less obvious. This includes things like pushing prayer off to a more convenient time or missing church to attend a soccer game.

Even when we set our plans for the day, can we really say they are made with Jesus at the front of our minds? It is ironic that the most positive and permanent force we have in our existence, Jesus, is the one we seem to push off to a more convenient time.

It is not that most of us are bad or terrible sinners. We haven't made Jesus more of a priority. Life gets in the way and becomes more important. This is the mistake we make. We are always waiting for tomorrow when today is a better day.

In thinking about the man in the bed, I ponder a thought I had once heard: *Jesus is all we need.* The more I thought about the man in the bed, it was also *all he had.*

That's the point of Jesus: What else do we have that will be with us from the beginning to the end of our lives on earth? Life here on earth can be boiled down to this point.

Over the years and centuries, much has been made and said about Jesus. Strong and well-thought-out theological ideas have been expressed. These are all nice, but do they inspire us to make Jesus everything?

Recently, while sitting on the beach, reading Karl Barth's *Epistle to the Romans,* I noticed that it took me 15 minutes to digest one paragraph. Barth is the most important Protestant theologian of the twentieth century. Indeed, he is one that every theological student will have to study at some point. His wording is complicated and extraordinarily dense, leading to an exciting but challenging effort to understand what he has to say about Jesus.

Mining these valuable insights is complex and cumbersome. For many, the great theologian Barth becomes inaccessible. This is also true for many other worthy and great theological writers, making theological study primarily an academic exercise. Jesus isn't this complicated, and each person has their own individual path to Jesus.

There is a strong need to move Jesus to the kitchen table. For many of the people I talk with and who give their thoughts, Jesus isn't an academic or theological exercise. They simply would love to be closer to Jesus.

Frankly, to have a great relationship with Jesus, all that is required is to simply have faith in Jesus as Lord and Savior, who loves us and wants the best for everyone. There is no pre-scribed formula for achieving this faith. It is acquired different-ly, person by person.

Each of our relationships with Jesus is very personal. It is sometimes developed through a crisis and other times through slow, steady steps. Regardless, each person desires to arrive at a place of faith, even in protest.

We all see and find Jesus in many different ways. And Jesus will meet us where we are.

So while I love reading Barth, I don't read his thoughts be-cause I agree with everything he has to say. He expands my mind to think about Jesus and helps me to know Jesus. I know this is one way I grow closer to Jesus, but I also know my way won't always help others. And I am sure Barth would be more than satisfied with this viewpoint. For others, this is not their entry into discovering Jesus.

And while I love to talk to professors of theology, I don't agree with everything they have to say. I listen to them because, like bumblebees, they drop pollen into my thoughts that ex-pand my relationship and understanding of Jesus. And each of my professors would be happy with that answer as well. This is my personal journey and the walk I walk with Jesus. Others have their own walk in faith.

I have also found that judging other people's paths to Jesus is and has been counterproductive. Instead, our task as minis-ters and theologians is to guide, not judge or demand. We need to be helpers as Jesus does His work.

I love to tweet on Twitter theological questions, like *Who is Jesus to you?* And always, I see an extraordinary outpouring of answers, far more significant than when I post any of my other reflections. They are beautiful responses to the question *Who is Jesus to you?*

It has made me study why this question makes people share not academically but with profound guttural expressions. They usually aren't judgmental responses: They are individuals sharing their joy. They love Jesus.

The one I found most remarkable, written by many, was *Jesus is everything.* It is a simple response that reveals so much about their relationship with Jesus. This response tells me about their experience with Jesus. Somewhere in either their distant or recent past, Jesus called them and helped them.

These encounters weren't made up but so extraordinarily personal and intimate that people have let go of worldly trusts and submitted to Jesus (much like the man in the bed in his last moments).

In this simple statement, we see the perfect definition of faith. People who say *Jesus is everything* rely on Jesus for all the times of their lives. When they need help, they seek Jesus. When they are content, they thank Jesus. This statement doesn't mean they don't fail, for indeed they do. It doesn't mean they are perfect, for none are. It simply means that their guttural response is to seek Jesus. I am sure they all would want to be better. And to be better, they know to stay focused on Jesus as *their everything.*

So for some, reading Barth is an excellent exercise in discovering how to feel about Jesus. Indeed, the professors of theology are valuable in helping frame thoughts and to think critically about Jesus. Minsters who guide and nurture more robust relationships with Jesus are wonderful hands-on helpers for Jesus.

But Jesus is always doing the hard work to help us with our faith. His efforts are always different for each individual because Jesus meets each of us where we are. Our task is to answer Jesus's calling and to move toward making *Jesus our everything*. The choice Jesus is asking each of us to make every day.

1

Jesus: The Way, the Truth, and the Life

Jesus answered, "I am the Way and the Truth and the Life. No one comes to the Father except through Me."

—John 14:6

Imagine if a person stood up and stated they are *the way, the truth, and the life (John 14:6).* We would look at them like they were crazy. Yet Jesus said this fundamental statement of our faith to the 12 apostles 2,000 years ago. He not only said it, but Jesus also made this statement boldly by adding, *No one comes to the Father except through Me.* If we had been present when Jesus made this statement 2,000 years ago, would we have believed Him? Or would we have thought, *This is a presumptuous statement for someone to make?*

Even earlier in the Gospel of John, as Jesus is talking with the apostles, He makes another bold and direct statement by saying, *You believe in God; believe also in Me (John 14:1).* Imagine someone in our friend group standing up at a party and saying something like this. We might either start laughing or become put off. Yet our faith tells us Jesus can make these statements because He undeniably is *the Way, the Truth, and the Life.*

Recognizing Jesus

Earlier in this meeting, Jesus had told the 12 apostles, *You know the way to the place where I am going (John 14:4).*

The apostle Thomas, always the curious and doubtful one, asks Jesus: *Lord, we don't know where You are going, so how can we know the way?* (John 14:5).

Jesus replies: *If you really know Me, you will know My Father as well. From now on, you do know Him and have seen Him. (John 14:7)*

There is the answer for us as well in Jesus's reply to Thomas: *If you really know Me,* we will know the way. To believe Jesus is *the Way, the Truth, and the Life,* we must really know and experience Jesus.

It is easy for us to look at this story of doubt by the apostles and say, *How could they not really know Jesus?* They had spent many months with Jesus, watching Him cast out evil spirits, heal people, and miraculously change people's lives. What makes the lack of believing by the apostles even more remarkable is that all of the evil spirits Jesus encountered along His journey knew who He was immediately. Yet those close to Him were still trying to grasp who Jesus was.

Early in Jesus's ministry, He visited a synagogue in Capernaum and began to preach. As He was talking, a man possessed by an evil spirit said, *What do you want with us, Jesus of Nazareth? Have you come to destroy us? I know who you are—the Holy One of God (Mark 1:24).* This event occurred at the beginning of Jesus's earthly mission, and it was an evil spirit that was one of the first to know who Jesus was.

The irony here is that the 12, who had been close to Jesus, didn't recognize who and what Jesus was, yet evil spirits knew Jesus was the one who could destroy them. And that is the irony of our lives as well. We often fail to recognize Jesus and His impact on our lives.

The apostles were stuck in their worldly thinking about Jesus. They had assumed He was going to be an earthly king. They were trained from birth to only trust their senses and to be watchers of the ways of the world. What Jesus was to them was foreign and required a different way of viewing life. They desperately wanted to have faith, but the entanglements of the world and their previous lives prevented them from truly knowing Jesus.

It is easy to judge these 12 apostles as weak in their faith. Yet are we any different? Have we really given in to who Jesus is, or are we just simply wanting to believe? Not sure we can trust what Jesus has to offer.

We are first born of flesh, and to believe the statement, *I am the Way, the Truth, and the Life,* we need to be born again through the Holy Spirit.

When asked, *How can I believe who Jesus is, and how do I become born again?* My answer is that we all must experience and know about Jesus. When we first feel this question in our hearts, we should know it is a sign that Jesus is trying to reach us. In effect, Jesus is compelling us to come to Him.

To experience Jesus, we first need to talk to Jesus. This conversation with Jesus happens through our prayers and in the deepest thoughts of our minds. The more we give of ourselves in exchange with Jesus, the closer we will grow in believing and having faith in Jesus.

Each conversation will make us hungrier to know Jesus. It is not a *let's try this and see* conversation but a deeply rooted urge to be connected. The more intense the conversation with Jesus, the more intense Jesus's response. And these responses will always be unusual and deeply personal. At first, we will say to ourselves, *Was that Jesus?* The more we continue on this path, the stronger our faith becomes, eventually leading to a point when we no longer have doubt.

There is no formula for how long this takes, I might add. The process of developing a trusting faith varies from individual to individual. For some, a crisis brings about this point. For others, it is a long period of asking and observing.

Jesus and the Bible

To know and experience Jesus, we should also read the Bible. First and foremost is believing the words of the Bible. Know that every word in the Bible is from the breath of God. No, I don't personally believe God sat at the table and wrote the words. Instead, the Bible was written by people inspired by the Holy Spirit. Others believe God physically wrote the Bible. And they may be right. Arguing this point is moot because we still end up in the same place; the Bible is the Holy Words of God.

As faithful Christians, we should always believe the Bible is God-breathed words of life. Many refer to the Bible as a book, and academia will refer to the Bible as *the text*. Neither is correct. Lowering the Bible to these human terms devalues the Bible. It removes the Bible from being sacred to an ordinary piece of literature.

The Bible is, in its current format, a book for the benefit of our understanding, another way God meets us where we are. In previous centuries, the Bible has existed on scrolls made of plant material. Even today, we have the Bible on our phones or even audiobooks and audiotapes. Regardless of the medium, it remains God's words for humankind.

Sure, some take the Bible literally, and others take the Bible metaphorically, causing great *human* debate. Some will even try to disprove the Bible by doing extensive historical research. This is completely missing the point and superfluous. The Bible is a multidimensional medium designed by God to deliver His message to humankind.

For example, let's unpack *the talking snake in the Garden of Eden.* Did the snake really talk, or was this metaphorical? Literalists will object to any metaphorical interpretation and can get highly offended. Those with a metaphorical bent will say the *talking snake* is used to make the story easier to remember. Historians will even research to see if any reptile was ever able to talk. This debate misses the point of the story. The story's message about the talking snake in the garden is straightforward: *Do God's will and not what you want.* This is the point about reading the Bible: We *all* (and I can't be more emphatic) enter the Bible differently. It is not who's right about how they enter the Bible. It's about how each of us experiences God's revelation through the words of the Bible.

While we are talking about the Bible, we also need to discuss the Holy Spirit. When reading the Bible, ask the Spirit to be with you. Magical things will happen if you fully bring the Holy Spirit into your reading of the Bible. The Spirit will enlighten the Bible for you and draw you in deeper each time.

The point of bringing up the Bible's importance is when we read Jesus say, *I am the Way, the Truth and the Life; we* should believe the words because they come from the Bible. We don't have to be born two thousand years ago to hear and experience Jesus! He is alive today, through the Bible.

The second necessary mindset in understanding that Jesus is *the Way, the Truth, and the Life* is to move from following the world to following the words of Jesus. The Bible, especially the four Gospels, gives us Jesus's direction and requirements.

I am sure you have noticed the news we get every day always seems to have the tone of bias reflecting the author's point of view. The ways of the world are always frail and fragile. What was good yesterday is wrong today, making actual truth from the world extraordinarily elusive. This is where the words of Jesus fill in the gaps. Instead of trusting the world, we should turn to Jesus to find the truth.

I tried a radical approach to this just as I entered theological school a decade ago. I put away newspapers, avoided the news on television and also the radio. I completely turned my eyes away from the world. (The only exception was following my beloved Boston sports teams!)

What I discovered at the end of a year of removing myself from the world was that I was more productive in my studies and relationships.

There was no detrimental aspect in my life. It allowed my mind to focus more closely on the ways of Jesus. My focus completely changed how I viewed life. After people heard that I did this, they would ask me, *How did you survive?* or *What did you miss?* I did survive, and I didn't miss anything!

This process led to more praying and to watching Jesus answer my prayers. My daily routine changed to having a *Jesus-first* mindset. During this period, I read the Bible from cover to cover. I was able to study hard and get good grades. My eyes turned to Jesus, and the world became an afterthought. I literally missed nothing important.

During this year, I discovered that Jesus was a more reliable compass and far more forgiving than the world at large. Today when I read the news, I feel the tug of the world. Sometimes the news makes me angry or propels me into the drama of people I don't even know. Usually, I have to sit down and recenter myself to stave off the effects.

I see the effect of the world's divisiveness in politics and the national media. People only listen to the truth that supports their agenda and then echo this truth to other like-minded people, creating a gulf between well-intentioned groups. I often find myself considered too liberal for conservatives and too conservative for liberals because of my insistence on seeking the real truth—just where I want to be.

Believing in the sacredness of the Bible is an excellent aid in experiencing and knowing Jesus. It also helps filter out the truth about life and, most importantly, how to know Jesus better.

Jesus Is the Way

So what does Jesus specifically mean when He exclaims, *I am the Way, and the Truth and the Life*? How are we to understand each aspect, and what is Jesus asking of us? Let's start with *the Way*.

As stated before, Thomas in John 14:5 says, *Lord, we don't know where You are going, so how can we know the way?* Thomas, the doubting Thomas, is looking in the wrong direction. Thomas is looking for a defined destination, a physical place to arrive.

Yet even in his doubting of this statement, Thomas knows one thing for sure. Jesus is the Lord. His very first word to Jesus is to acknowledge the primary position of Jesus as the Lord.

Thomas's inquiry is sincere and, certainly from a worldly aspect, legitimate. For Jesus, *the Way* is a very different meaning than a destination. Instead, it is more about *how* and not *where*. This distinction is essential for us—being a follower of Jesus isn't about where we are going. Instead, it is about how we follow Jesus.

All of Jesus's actions and his ways are focused on serving the Father with obedience. How He lived and thought was always for the benefit of the Father and His neighbor.

Consider the things Jesus said and did: His walk to the cross, the lonely night in the garden to fully accept God's will, His expressions of forgiveness, and His even-handedness with all He met, even those of ill repute. Jesus gave everyone a fair and even chance. Jesus himself lived the life He was preaching. What Jesus asks for from us is the same as what Jesus did Himself. He served rather than being served.

This is one aspect of what *the Way* means. In a more sacred way, Jesus is also telling the apostles that only through Him can we receive the bounty of grace. Jesus is telling them, He is the intermediary of God. After all, Jesus is the one with His own blood that opened the way for humankind to go to God because of His actions on the cross.

Jesus as the Way is the one who purifies us when we encounter God. This is why when we say, *In Jesus's name, we pray,* Jesus becomes our way to God.

In verse 10 of Chapter 14 of John, Jesus says: *Don't you believe that I am in the Father, and that the Father is in Me? The words I say to you I do not speak on My own authority. Rather, it is the Father, living in Me, who is doing His work (John 14:10).* Note that Jesus is in God, and God is in Jesus.

But also note the message of humble obedience on Jesus's part when He says, *I do not speak on My own authority.* And then when He points out, *It is the Father, living in Me, who is doing His work (John 14:10).* This is another aspect of *the Way* that Jesus is pointing out. To follow Jesus, we must be humble and let the work of the Lord be done through and within us.

Jesus Is the Truth

Jesus also states that He is *the Truth*. So why is Jesus saying this? He is simply asking us to turn from what we see in the world and be honest with ourselves. Jesus knows the truth of the world is elusive and tainted. He also knows the stories we tell ourselves and others always have a tincture of falsehood. To find the real truth, Jesus wants us to be pointed directly to His words.

Recently, in our political discourse, we have heard the words *fake news.* Now, this isn't a new concept. Perhaps using the term *fake news* is, but throughout history, facts have always been distorted. It is part of the natural human condition. What we get from the world is usually not the complete truth.

We see it every day: Salespeople will bend the facts about their products. People don't always reveal everything when they are looking for help. Certainly, you have heard, *The check is in the mail.*

This is part of Jesus's point: We can trust His words and His impact on our lives. Human history is extraordinarily elusive, but the Word of God is never elusive.

Jesus also asks us to evaluate ourselves honestly and openly. Part of doing this is mirroring Jesus's behavior in all things. For instance, it is easy to love our family and friends. But can we love our enemy? What stories do we create to prevent this? Are we being objective? Are we really hurt at a slight, or have we made the slight too big?

Part of the reason Jesus says, *I am the Truth*, is Jesus is asking us to measure all that we say, think, and do against His example. We have all heard the phrase, *What would Jesus do?* Knowing and mirroring *What Jesus would do* will always show us the path of the truth. Using the term *What would Jesus do* moves away from the short-term benefit for ourselves to the longer-term benefit of being aligned with Jesus.

When Jesus says, *I am the Truth,* it is multifaceted. Jesus wants us to measure everything we see or read against His example and that of the Word of God. In doing so, we learn to discover what is real and what is an illusion. When we do this, a veil is removed from our eyes and thoughts.

Then we will find the real *truth* about ourselves and the world around us. To discover this *real truth*, we must also bury our wants and rid ourselves of our desires, turning everything over to Jesus's way. The cleansing of ourselves is the hardest part of finding the *real truth*.

Jesus Is the Life

Next, Jesus tells us He is *the Life*. Jesus created our eternal life through the cross. Having faith in Jesus's resurrection is paramount to understanding eternal life and Jesus as the Life.

Having faith that Jesus is God is also part of the reason Jesus says, *I am the life.* In the Gospel of John, Jesus says *I Am* seven times. This is not a coincidental inclusion. Numbers mean a lot in the Bible. And the number seven means *divine perfection.* Whenever we see seven or a series of seven items in the Bible, we are being told that what we are reading is important and associated with God. In this case, through the repetition of *I Am* in the Gospel of John, we get a very clear statement about Jesus's divinity. He is God.

When we go back to the Old Testament in Exodus 3:14, God says to Moses: *I Am who I Am.* God is responding to Moses's question of *Who are You?* God answers by saying *I Am.* This is how God refers to God. But it is also a parallel to what Jesus is saying: *I am the life.*

Believing fully that Jesus is God is critical to our understanding of the statement, *I am the life.* Jesus is the creator of life, and all that exists. The first verse in the Gospel of John says, *In the beginning was the Word, and the Word was with God, and the Word was God.* This verse is as important as any line in the four Gospels. Notice the word, *Word.* This is a direct reference to Jesus. Let's reread this line substituting Jesus's name: *In the beginning was Jesus, and Jesus was with God, and Jesus was God.* Jesus was with and is God from the beginning!

Knowing this changes Jesus from being an earthly entity to being the creator of all things, who works in concert with the Father and the Holy Spirit. When we fully take on this view, we can now choose to follow Jesus, who created all that existed and died to redeem us from our sins or follow a different path. This choice is the single most important choice we have to make in our lives. *Choose Jesus!*

This is *the Life* Jesus is talking about: a life of knowing, following, and experiencing the Great Creator of all things.

To all these things, we have a choice: We can choose our way, our truth, and our life or Jesus's. Jesus will always compel us to choose *His way, His truth, and His life.* And know this: Jesus will never stop asking us to follow Him. Jesus won't give up until we know *Jesus is everything.*

2

Jesus Meets Us Where We Are

The grace of the Lord Jesus Christ be with your spirit. Amen

—Philippians 4:23

Sitting in a Bible study group, I watched two men angrily arguing about who Jesus was. One man vehemently argued that Jesus was the Lamb of God. The other man argued that Jesus was Lord and Savior. Back and forth they went, citing Bible verses and quoting famous theologians but never agreeing.

I wanted to blurt out that they were both right. Then it occurred to me they were making a statement about who Jesus was to them individually, afraid that if they gave into each other, then Jesus would change for them. I am sure for the reader or listener, this argument seems silly because of the two men's insistence on their point of view.

It is not so much whether they were right individually but a reflection of how Jesus meets us as individuals. Jesus enters our lives in many different ways. Jesus is constantly trying to steer us based on who and where we are in our lives. Perhaps it is a time we need to grow spiritually. Or maybe Jesus is trying to get us to grow in our service to others. The many ways Jesus becomes our everything are both undefinable and infinitely varied. Trying to define Jesus in our lives is always a personal task for us and not always the answer for others.

Pastor Lou: Jesus's Sled Dog

Pastor Lou is a perfect example of a person who has been affected by our Lord and Savior. Like many of us, Lou started out seeking a life through a professional career. He was always somewhat successful but not always satisfied. At first, Lou was a manager of people in a business environment; then, he turned to construction. As his early life unfurled, he lived in many different parts of our country.

Lou always felt the tug of Jesus, sometimes answering the call and other times putting Jesus aside to continue to pursue a career, never really becoming satisfied, just constantly moving down the life he perceived was best.

Over time, he answered the call from Jesus, which sent Lou to inquire about becoming a pastor. He studied and took the courses that the United Methodist Church suggested he take, eventually becoming a pastor for the United Methodist Church. Still, Lou didn't get what he was looking for. As new assignments arose, Lou always seemed to be passed by. He struggled to get the recognition he deserved, always preaching at smaller churches and having to scrape by.

When a major housing crisis in New Jersey occurred, caused by Super Storm Sandy, the church asked Lou to head up the construction effort to rebuild homes for the displaced people. Naturally, Lou excelled and put over 200 families back into rebuilt or new homes. In fact, Lou's cost of construction was a fraction of what other agencies spent.

Along the way, Lou also ministered to the displaced families and individuals, giving them words of hope and wise counsel. Lou not only was their construction manager, but he also became their pastor during difficult times. When I talked with

Lou about this secondary work, he beamed with joy. This was what he sought, to help others spiritually. In all the moments of his life, being there for others gives him the greatest joy. This was where Jesus was sending Lou as a hands-on helper for those both spiritually and materially poor.

Lou is one of those people you can call at two in the morning. No matter the crisis, he lives to serve. He is a sled dog, and his joy comes from helping. Lou is not sophisticated in speech, nor is he concerned with outward appearances. Lou doesn't get great joy from what he accomplishes. His joy comes from helping people out.

When rebuilding hurricane-savaged homes was finished, Lou hoped for a more prominent role or a bigger church. Instead, he was given three tiny churches to pastor, causing him to travel extensively on Sunday mornings to deliver three sermons. Lou found himself constantly on the road helping serve these three small churches while watching other people receive assignments in churches that would provide a more stable life. Over time, Lou got worn down and prayed for direction. Lou had hit another dead end in his life.

Lou always was a person who prayed frequently. He had prayed heavily over the previous four years, always wondering why everyone else seemed to get ahead. Lou was a good soldier for Jesus and always jumped at any chance to help. Yet, it appeared he was always unnoticed. It seemed that no matter what Lou did, it wasn't where Jesus wanted him to be.

Lou felt Jesus ask him to start a church. He found a building and started to recruit a flock. He held Sunday service and grew a small following. He continued on the side to do construction management to help pay his bills. Just after he started the church, COVID-19 emerged, and once again, Lou had what some would say was another setback.

Lou, as always, didn't give up; ways to help showed up in his life. He saw a need to fill in feeding shut-ins—those who could no longer get served because of the new regulations caused by COVID-19. As usual, Lou found a solution.

Lou also works as a chaplain for local police departments and is the chaplain for the New Jersey State Police. Lou gets calls late at night or early in the morning to help with difficult situations, like homicides or even helping members of the various departments to deal with depression. Lou is well aware that those who serve are frequently put into life or death situations and need to know God is involved.

Lou also started a prayer ministry. Each morning six days a week, he texts prayers and a two- to three-paragraph reflection to hundreds of people in his community, all to help them start the day centered on the Lord. Each of us who receives these messages is grateful for what Lou has to say each morning.

On Christmas 2020, Lou handed out blankets and coats to the homeless in his local community. In the cold, Lou was standing there with a smile and an ear for the people in need. Many people miss this about Lou: He doesn't want praise. He wants to help. Lou is a sincere and humble person whose first love is Jesus.

Lou has worked hard to serve Jesus, and it has taken him a lifetime to find out where Jesus wanted him. In the years I have known Lou, this is his most joyful time. He will never be rich or famous. Lou will never become a great preacher for a mega-church. Instead, Lou will serve thousands of police officers who need comfort. He will feed hundreds each week, text hundreds of us each morning to lift our souls, and nourish a small congregation with the words of the Gospel on Sunday. Even state governors call Lou for prayers.

Jesus had asked Lou to *feed My lambs*, similar to the request Jesus made to Peter 2,000 years earlier. Lou found joy by completely giving in to Jesus. Lou finally dropped his ambitions and hunt for relevancy from the world. Now he lives a life he always desired. It took a few years, but Lou is a spiritually rich person.

For Lou, Jesus is one to serve, and through service, he finds his purpose. Lou loves to serve and help. Jesus is, to Lou, someone to help. And like an obedient follower, Lou helps. Jesus is different to Lou than other people. Lou's relationship with Jesus goes something like this: *What's next boss? I am ready to go!* What Lou needs from Jesus is a job to do and a few kind moments here and there. That's all, nothing fancy. Like a good lead sled dog, Lou wants to pull the sled. After a lifetime of trying to find out where he should go, Lou gave in and wholly followed Jesus.

The Apostle John: The Son of Love

Another person who had a very different relationship with Jesus was the apostle John. John met Jesus through John the Baptist. Early in Jesus's mission on earth, Jesus walked near John the Baptist and the future apostle John. As Jesus passed them, John the Baptist said, *Behold, the Lamb of God,* making John curious and wanting to follow Jesus. Andrew, another future apostle, joined in. Jesus, sensing them following Him, turned and said, *What are you seeking?* In turn, they asked where he was staying. Instead of answering this question, Jesus invited them to follow Him, and off they went. Later, Andrew would get Peter and introduce him to Jesus. Likewise, John went and brought his brother, the future apostle James, to meet Jesus. This was how the early selection of the 12 apostles occurred.

Back to the story of John. The future apostle was an ambitious person and was always looking for glory. He also could be loud and boisterous, as was his brother, James. In the early days, Jesus called them the *sons of thunder.*

John mistakenly fell into the trap the world set out, that of seeking personal glory and fame through Jesus. John was constantly looking for the next big thing. Initially, this is what he thought following Jesus would provide. If John couldn't get his way, he could get loud and pushy. To fully achieve his purpose in life, he needed to be softened and redirected. Jesus saw this in John and slowly began to chisel him.

In one particular story, John asked Jesus if he and his brother could sit next to him when Jesus's kingdom would start. Needless to say, Jesus was a little taken aback, and the other ten apostles got mad at this brazen request by John.

By the way, John's mother also went to Jesus and asked the same thing. This might be the first recorded account of a *helicopter parent*. In both cases, Jesus replied that they didn't know what they were asking, explicitly asking John in Matthew 20:22, *Are you willing to take the suffering I am about to take?* At this point, John wasn't. John's first goal was ambition, and serving humanity wasn't yet on his agenda.

Another example of John's misplaced exuberance occurred as Jesus and the apostles were making the last and fateful trip into Jerusalem. They passed a town in Samaria that would not accept Jesus. John and his brother asked Jesus if they could bring down fire and destroy the city. Jesus gave John a stern look and rebuked him. Jesus wasn't interested in destroying a town. This violent act of retribution was not Jesus's way. Once again, John had let his zeal and quick-to-anger attitude suggest an action that would have felt good for an instance but left a blemish on the ministry of Jesus.

Jesus kept chiseling John's brashness. But it wasn't until after Jesus's death on the cross and subsequent resurrection that John got the point. As followers of Jesus, we do not become kings. We become servants. Our real treasure doesn't lie in our power and fame but in His service. John would go on to serve for many years. Tradition holds that John was the last to die of the original 12. Over time, he did lose his brashness and ambition.

As Christian persecution mounted in the mid-first century, many of the original apostles left Jerusalem and spread the message of Jesus throughout the Mediterranean world. John was no exception. His ministry was centered in the country known today as Turkey, more specifically Ephesus.

Much of John's preaching in later life centered on love—a message he lived so much that instead of being one of the *sons of thunder*, he became called one of the *sons of love*.

When we read accounts of the second-century Christian leaders, we find a powerful link back to John. It seems that John had quite a following after he left Jerusalem. Polycarp, a writer and Christian philosopher of the second century, was a protégé of John's. Polycarp's writings are among some of the earliest Christian literature to survive. It is through Polycarp we can experience authentic John thoughts: love first!

Polycarp is also important and very exciting when it comes to connecting to the historical Jesus. His writings exist when few from that period survived. In these writings, we can discover a lot about John. This is why it is so important because it provides a direct link back to Jesus.

John told and taught Polycarp about Jesus. Through the writings of Polycarp, we have an eyewitness to one of the original apostles, who in turn was closely connected to Jesus. For those who need more authentic proof that Jesus lived, Polycarp provides this evidence.

When John first started as one of Jesus's 12, he was young, brash, ambitious, and quick to anger. These qualities weren't aligned with the message of Jesus. John needed to change, and Jesus never gave up on John. Jesus saw John's potential, which was why John was selected to be part of the 12. Jesus was what John needed.

Without the mistakes John made early in his time with Jesus, John wouldn't have learned what he needed. Like many of us, at first, we have our *go-to* responses, mostly from what we have learned from the ways of the world. John thought Jesus was going to be a worldly king and wanted to be part of that kingdom. He thought that there would be riches and fame. He was ambitious and chased this dream. He didn't mind who he stepped on to achieve this fame. He was after what the world told him to do.

What Jesus did was change John to see it wasn't about himself. Life was about loving God and his neighbor without thoughts of personal gain. In doing this, John gained everything and lost his thunder. He gained a heart of love.

John's and Lou's journeys to a life where Jesus is everything were different. Lou is a very ordinary man trying to make a life for himself. Lou kept looking in the wrong places and kept looking for validation of what he achieved. It wasn't until he was forced to rely on Jesus entirely that he found his true calling. His validation came from Jesus.

John was extraordinarily ambitious and believed his life's purpose was fame and glory. It took experiencing the death and resurrection of Jesus to see what he was seeking was to be a servant.

That is the point: All of us have a unique destiny and life purpose through Jesus, not through what the world tells us. Instead, what Jesus wants for and from us is discovered by listening closely to Jesus. When Jesus becomes everything to each of us, our journeys may be very different but will always be right for us.

3

Following Jesus Requires a Change in Our Lives

Whoever wants to be My disciple must deny themselves and take up their cross and follow Me.

—Mark 8:34

Near the end of Jesus's time on earth and post-resurrection, Jesus pulled Peter aside to talk with him. They had just finished breakfast, and Jesus said to Peter, *Simon son of John, do you love Me more than these? (John 21:15)*

What is curious about this statement is that Jesus used Simon's birth name. Early in His gathering of apostles, Jesus had changed Simon's name to Peter, translated to mean *the rock.* Studying curious items like this in the Bible is called exegesis or looking for a deeper meaning. In this case, Jesus was taking Peter back to his pre-Jesus days when he was a fisherman.

Why would Jesus do this, and why would He ask, *Do you love Me more than these?* Answering these questions will tell us what Jesus is up to in this conversation and the change He wants to make in Peter.

Jesus is subtly reminding Peter of his life pre-Jesus. Peter didn't have a bad life. He had a trade that provided him resources to live. Peter had his family and friends. He had a normal life.

After Jesus was crucified, surprisingly, we find Peter back in his old life. Likely, disappointed that things didn't work out as Peter expected. He had hoped the movement he joined following Jesus would get very big. When Jesus died, Peter felt something had come to an end. He returned to his old ways and life.

Earlier in this story about Jesus pulling Peter aside post-resurrection, Jesus was standing on the shore watching some of the apostles in a fishing boat, with Peter as the leader. Previously, Peter had told the apostles who were with him—Nathanael, Thomas, John, and James—that night he was going fishing, returning to his old life. The others volunteered to go with him.

They fished for a while and had nothing to show for their efforts. Their net was empty. As they returned to the shore, a man, who they did not recognize at first, was standing there waving to them. The man on the shore was Jesus, who said, *Friends, haven't you any fish?*

They replied, *No.*

Jesus, whom they still didn't recognize, then said, *Throw your net on the right side of the boat and you will find some. When they did, they were unable to haul the net in because of the large number of fish (John 21:6).*

Then one of the apostles recognized it was Jesus on the shore. Immediately, Peter noticed it was Jesus as well. Peter jumped in the water to hurry and greet Jesus. About one hundred yards offshore, the others guided the boat to shore, pulling the entire net of fish behind them.

When all got to the shore, they found a pit of coals with fish and bread cooking. Jesus asked them to bring some of the fish they caught. Peter hurriedly went back to the net and dragged it ashore. Then Jesus invited them to have breakfast with Him. Jesus broke the bread and handed it to them. He did the same with the fish. They were eating again with Jesus. This was the third time Peter and these apostles had seen Jesus post-resurrection.

Once again, Jesus had shown Peter his power and miraculously provided for him. Peter and his lack of faith had returned him to being Simon the fisherman. Not disappointed with Peter for his falling back into his old life, Jesus, one more time, provided sustenance for him. Another lesson for Peter about Jesus's persistence.

After this breakfast is when Jesus pulled Peter aside and asked the question: *Simon, son of John, do you love Me more than these?* Was Peter going to finally believe Jesus was the Lord and know that he must follow?

Jesus knew in a few days He was going to ascend into heaven, but first, He must convince Peter to be *the rock* and not Simon. Jesus knew Peter was His man. With this question, Jesus was prodding Peter to think about his future. Would Peter go back to his life as a fisherman, or would he go on to become *the rock* upon which Jesus would build the church? Could Peter change?

With His simple question of, *Do you love Me more than these?* Jesus is asking Peter if fitting in with his former friends is becoming more important than the mission of leading the group that would spread the earthly message of the Gospel? For those of us who know this story, it might be somewhat surprising Jesus would ask Peter these questions. And we may be surprised Peter didn't understand who and what Jesus was, even after being visited three times post-resurrection. We have had a similar experience, different, but Jesus has visited us.

Peter replies to Jesus, *Yes, I love You.*

Jesus then says, *Feed My lambs.* After which He asks Peter a second time, *Simon, son of John, do you love Me?*

And for a second time, Peter replies, *Yes, I love You.*

Again Jesus says, *Tend My sheep,* and repeats the question, *Do you love Me?*

Now Peter is thinking hard about why Jesus keeps asking him if he loves Him. Peter sits grieved and confused. In his mind, he was still tossing and turning about a complete commitment, torn by the familiar and a perceived safe life or moving down a path of fully committing to Jesus. Even in his last fishing expedition, Jesus fished for him.

This is an intense moment in his life; he knows that there is perceived certainty in staying where he is comfortable, fishing and socializing with his friends, and considering his time with Jesus as a nice life event. But Peter knows what Jesus is asking of him: to give all that up and believe in the mission of serving Jesus. He also knows this decision would lead to uncomfortable moments if he were going to achieve what Jesus was asking of him.

Torn, he sat silently, tossing the alternatives around. Peter had seen those who had attacked and threatened Jesus. In turn, he knew this would happen to him. He had a decision to make: *lead a mediocre comfortable life with few challenges or lead the extraordinary life Jesus was asking of him filled with difficult times.*

Three times Jesus asked this question, *Do you love Me?* When we see three in the Bible, it represents divine wholeness, completeness, and perfection. For instance, the resurrection took three days. There are three forms of God, called the Trinity. For this moment, three represents the completeness of Peter finally accepting his future.

We all know the end of this story: Peter changed and gave up being Simon and left his comfortable life. He did become the leader of the early Christians and braved many dangers. He would go on to oversee the development of the new church. A church that moved from being a small backwater sect in a remote part of the Roman Empire to an international following.

Later, Peter would leave his home city and go to Rome, then the center and ruling place of Western civilization, a place of difficulty. The ruling class was uncomfortable with this new way of life of following Jesus. Peter would have to deal with persecution and distrust. But it was in Rome where Peter would drop Jesus's pollen and help set off the great evangelistic expansion of the Christian way.

Despite the prevailing persecutions and distrust of Christianity from many in power, Peter strengthened the Christians then residing in Rome. He accomplished what Jesus saw in him, *the rock.* Peter became the first head of the church in Rome or the first Pope.

Peter, like Jesus, was sentenced to death by the leaders of Rome, and like Jesus was to be crucified. Peter, not feeling worthy enough to die precisely as Jesus had died, asked to be crucified upside down. He was crucified upside down and buried. His remains today are on the grounds where the Vatican sits, a historical fact confirmed in 1968.

Amazingly, the Roman leaders thought killing Peter would end the rise of Christianity. Instead, as we know today, Christianity blossomed. Like Peter, many others in these early days of Christianity would die because they refused to worship the Roman gods. The Roman leaders didn't stamp out Christianity; they gave people a martyr.

Peter achieved what Jesus asked of him. This story is also a story for us. Jesus is even asking for a change in each of us, which will move us from being comfortable to being challenged to do something different in our lives. The easy part is to know that Jesus loves us, and we all should. The harder task is to show we love Jesus and are willing to change and move faithfully to performing that which Jesus asks of us. Jesus is asking all of us, *Do you love Me more than these?*

Mother Teresa: Jesus's Little Flower

Mother Teresa had an experience similar to Peter's early in her life. As a young nun in 1946, situated in the lower Himalayas at the Loreto Convent, she began to have inner visions of talking with Jesus. Jesus was calling her from her safe sanctuary to help Calcutta's desperately poor, or in Hindu, Kalakatta. For this tiny woman, safely stowed away in a mountain enclave, her moving into abject poverty would be pretty shocking and disruptive.

Like Peter, Mother Teresa had a different name before she became a nun. Her name was Anjeze, meaning pure and delicate. In some quarters, it means *little flower*. Teresa was just that, tiny in physical terms, but had a giant and pure heart. In fact, in Teresa's vision, she heard Jesus call her His *little wife*.

Initially, Teresa felt unworthy. In her memoirs, she wrote that she told Jesus, *I can hardly grasp even half of what it is that you want. Go, Jesus, and look for a soul that is worthier and more generous.* For 13 months, she wrestled with Jesus, constantly feeling unworthy. Her final vision was that of Jesus saying to her, *I cannot go alone to the poor people; you carry Me with you to them.* Finally relenting in 1948, she headed to Calcutta and started her work, which lasted for 49 years, until her death.

During this long period, she often felt abandoned and suffered episodes of depression. Mother Teresa called this period *a terrible darkness and dryness.* She still kept a brave face but wrote privately, *People think that my faith, my hope, and my love are overflowing and that my intimacy with God and union fill my heart. If only they knew!* This persistent doubt was revealed after her death and as she was being examined for sainthood. For 49 years, she worked for the poor, and after her experience with Jesus in 1947, she never had another vision or contact with Jesus.

For 49 years, Mother Teresa worked with the poorest of the poor. Over time, her order grew; by 1996, over 5,000 nuns operated 500 plus missions in over 100 countries. Mother Teresa won the Nobel Peace Prize in 1979. This reluctant missionary, who was born in Macedonia, accomplished as much for Jesus as any person in the twentieth century; she was a reluctant and humble worker for Jesus, who had to change to achieve Jesus's mission for her.

Jesus Has an Adventure for Us

While the stories of Peter's and Mother Teresa's journeys in faith are different, they are also similar in the sense that Jesus asked both of them to take their faith journeys when they had their feet in two different worlds: the world of safety and the world of the divine. For Peter, it was retreating to his past life of being a fisherman and the comfort of friends. For Mother Teresa, it was the comfort of the known in a safe mountain hideaway.

Neither is without controversy. Peter denied Jesus three times before the cock crowed on the night Jesus was arrested and sentenced to die. Later in Peter's leadership, he would sometimes take positions that offered safety and avoided controversy. Mother Teresa could be harsh in her management style and was accused of not giving the best care to those in her care.

Like all followers of Jesus, they could fall short of their Christian values. In a time when the world too harshly judged their mistakes, Jesus continued to rely on them in their missions. This is the point about Jesus: He doesn't judge us by our past, reluctance to serve, or even our missteps. Unlike the world at large, Jesus knows our heart and forgives.

Peter had witnessed the events leading up to the crucifixion and the post-resurrection. He had seen the many miracles of Jesus. Peter denied knowing Jesus three times during that fateful period. Seeking to save himself, he walked away from all he had seen and experienced. He went back to fishing, only to have Jesus reinstate him as Peter, *the rock.*

Mother Teresa certainly knew that in the slums of Kalakatta, there was disease, violence, and a troubled group of people. She was safely tucked away in a remote part of the world where she taught. Jesus called her to move beyond the interior walls of safety to living the dream Jesus had for her.

Thankfully, they both answered Jesus's call. Life didn't get easier for either. Peter would later also get crucified. Mother Teresa likewise suffered from depression and doubt. The lives they changed and saved were legendary—both left legacies of being Jesus's servants.

For us today, Jesus is calling us to do something different for the Kingdom. Jesus wants us to leave the world of a comfortable known to a grander journey in the unknown.

Jesus is always knocking at our door, asking us to cross over and direct our lives differently. We will argue and even ignore these calls. Some will answer, and some will seek temporary safety. What Jesus is asking of us is to be remarkable and not live the illusionary ways of the world.

For Jesus to be our everything, we simply have to give up the comfortable lives we have self-created and live His adventure of faith He has for us.

4

Our Relationship with Jesus Requires a Courageous Faith

Jesus replied, "You do not realize now what I am doing, but later you will understand."

—John 13:7

In the morning, Les prayed for his wife, who was to have major surgery that day. Worried about her health and the outcome, Les fervently prayed for her safety and wisdom for the doctors.

Later, Les received a call informing him that a life-changing business transaction he needed to be completed was in jeopardy. Les thought to himself, *That is the answer to my prayer, more troubles?*

Resolutely, Les asked for a meeting later that morning to meet the potential buyer and resolve the issue. During the meeting, it was revealed that the buyer was changing the terms and wanted a new deal. Les refused and patiently stated that they had a deal. Les then logically went through the numbers, showing the buyer why it was a good deal for both of them. He received no response from the buyer.

On top of his wife's medical condition, he now had the burden of a broken business arrangement, which would harm his future—an amazing coincidence. Frustrated, Les added to his prayer.

Later that afternoon, his wife went into surgery, and for the first time that day, Les had nothing to do but sit in a waiting room. He settled back in a chair to center himself and breathe deeply. He prayed again.

An hour later, he received word that the buyer had agreed with Les and his important business transaction was going forward.

A few minutes later, he saw the surgeon approach him. Nervously he stood up to hear the news. The surgeon told him his wife's condition wasn't as serious as they had thought. The result of the surgery was a success.

After a long day of turmoil, in an instant, everything changed. What seemed dire wasn't. His prayers were answered.

Being Patient in Prayer

Many times when we pray, the answer doesn't come immediately. Even when we desperately wait, things can often worsen, leaving us feeling our prayers have gone unanswered. However, every prayer said with faith is *always* answered. Yes, every faithful prayer. It may not be the answer wanted but the answer needed.

As we wait, if we don't maintain a courageous faith, we will sink further into the abyss. Waiting is a period that can test our faith. During these times, faithful patience and courage are just as important as the prayer itself.

A helpful thought I have found that works is not to worry about the answer that will be given; instead, have a courageous faith knowing Jesus is involved.

In these times of stress, knowing that Jesus is listening and hearing is vital. We must stay riveted on seeking Jesus and stay focused on the Word of God. Waiting becomes a time to test our thoughts and see how they measure up to the words of Jesus. If our thoughts are tied closely to Jesus, we are on the right course and only need to wait.

Never continue in a direction if it is not God's will or Jesus's way. The hole will only get deeper. No matter how much our actions might soothe the moment, if it is unholy, selfish, or desperate, we will find ourselves off the course of Jesus's plan and derail our prayers—forcing us deeper into despair.

Jesus's Courage Walking to the Cross

As both human and God, Jesus mirrored for us how to be during difficult days. Think about the period of the crucifixion. There is no historical event more traumatic than the three days of the crucifixion and resurrection. In Jesus's humanness, He struggled to keep His bearing. Before He knelt alone in the garden to pray, He told three of the apostles in Matthew 26:38, *My soul is very sorrowful, even to death; remain here and watch with Me (ESV)*. In these words, we can see Jesus's humanness and desperate struggle to make sense out of what He should do next.

And He did, what we should all do: He prayed. Jesus prayed for guidance three times, kneeling in the garden of Gethsemane. He did not seek His way out of the problematic situation. Very revealing was His asking God in Matthew 26:39, *My Father, if it is possible, let this cup pass from Me, nevertheless, not as I will, but as You will (ESV)*.

These are amazing words of submission and desire to do only what God wants in a remarkably difficult situation. Jesus was being honest with God; He knew the following hours would be extraordinarily difficult, and He wanted to do something else. Yet Jesus uses an important word, *nevertheless*, to express that no matter how desperate He is, Jesus only wants to do what God wants. He is not afraid to reveal His desperation, nor is he unwilling to follow the course set out for Him. He prayed that night three times, and three times He got the same answer: He must proceed. There would be no compromising of God's will.

We all know the rest of this story: Jesus is arrested, later to be humiliated, beaten to near death, forced to carry a heavy cross, and finally nailed through the wrists and ankles—left hanging on a cross to suffocate. This is as difficult a set of events as any human will ever have to endure, but Jesus prevailed.

This is the great story of Easter. Jesus rose from the grave, defeating death and absorbing all our sins, a heavy burden carried by Jesus for our salvation. No other feat in history compares to this accomplishment.

For 40 days after, Jesus continued here on earth to tie up a few loose ends and then ascend to heaven. In His humanness, I am sure Jesus was relieved that He followed God's plan by going to the cross. He passed a difficult trial for God and humankind, and on the other side of this event, Jesus as a human knew He did what He had to do.

It is the courage and patient faith of this story we should not forget. Jesus knew He had to go through difficult times and face unrelenting foes. Personally, for us, we may have similar moments, not as dire but similar. There will be those moments when we have to have a courageous faith, identical to Jesus's.

As we face our times of tumult, this is the lesson we should follow as well. Perhaps a medical procedure will be on the horizon or owning up to a mistake we made. We can and should pray. We should also be willing to do what Jesus wants us to do and not what we want to do. Even though things may worsen and not get better for a time, Jesus has a plan for us. A courageous faith helps us stick to the plan.

Faith Made Her Well

Sometimes our turmoil in life is not the direct result of anything we did but that of circumstance. Occasionally, we are innocent victims thrust into the middle of an enormous problem, which requires us to stay close to Jesus and be courageous with our faith.

A remarkable story of courageous faith occurs in Mark 5:25–34. Here we find a woman who has suffered from chronic bleeding for 12 years. For 12 years, she spent all the money she had on doctors, only to have her condition worsen.

The woman was beset with a disease that caused her to bleed continuously. The disease was not caused by her actions, and she was desperate. The more she tried to heal herself, the worse things got.

In the first century, a person with a chronic bleeding disease would have been considered *spiritually unclean* and not welcome in her community. Isolated and sinking into a never-ending state of decline, she became desperate.

She recently had heard about Jesus and said to herself, *If I just touch His clothes, I will be healed (Mark 5:28).* At this moment, after many years of struggling, she felt she had found her answer. After 12 lonely and difficult years, she finally had hope.

Her next step required extreme courage and persistence. She had to get close to Jesus. No easy task as a diseased woman. Women in the first century had very few rights; talking to Jesus was not the appropriate social protocol. She certainly would not be welcomed in the first century to be part of a crowd seeking Jesus.

When Jesus came to her town, He was like a modern-day rock star; a crowd encircled Him, wanting to see and hear Jesus. Despite her social status and illness, she began to make her way through the very thick crowd. Looking for small breaks in the crowd, she patiently and persistently moved closer to Jesus. Then she saw she could reach out and touch His clothes. As she did, in an instant, she felt a powerful healing of her body and was no longer trapped by her disease. She was freed.

Jesus felt the power leave Him, turned around, and hurriedly asked, *Who touched My clothes? (Mark 5:30).* When His disciples heard this, they were surprised Jesus would ask this question because the crowd was so thick around Him.

The woman fell to Jesus's feet and told Him it was her. Jesus replied, *Daughter, your faith has healed you. Go in peace and be freed from your suffering (Mark 5:34).* Her faith had made her well—a remarkable statement of compassion from Jesus.

She had performed no tremendous physical or mental task. She had a courageous and persistent faith that Jesus was the answer. She had never given up on her task to be healed. Her final heroic and faith-filled effort to fight her way through a crowd to simply touch Jesus's cloak is what healed her.

In our prayers for relief, we will often experience temporary periods of things getting worse, not better. Many people I talk with have experienced these short-term setbacks, even immediately after an intense prayer for relief. And this is where courage and enduring faith, like the bleeding woman's, needs to be maintained.

The bleeding woman had done nothing wrong in her life yet found herself crippled by circumstance. When she discovered Jesus, she knew ardently He was her answer. It isn't that Jesus wanted her to suffer; he didn't. This was her faith journey, a life lesson in how to be freed from this life's natural afflictions. We can be sure from this point forward, Jesus was everything to the woman.

Part of our journey with Jesus is doing the tough things to resolve difficult situations. These difficult times are part of our journey with Jesus, times when we walk His path, and we become strengthened in our faith. We learn to rely on Jesus for everything to get us through the storms of our lives.

5

We Are Worthy Because Jesus Makes Us Worthy

For we are God's handiwork, created in Christ Jesus to do good works, which God prepared in advance for us to do.

—Ephesians 2:10

When I told my wife, Connie, that I was writing this book, she reminded me that not everybody feels worthy of Jesus. She's right. Many do not feel worthy. And this thought is one that I think has to be immediately and entirely dismissed in any person's mind. All people are worthy of Jesus!

Other theologians constantly challenge my view that all people are worthy as being too rosy an outlook of humankind. But I stand firm. Everyone is worthy of Jesus. The only condition for this worthiness is that we have faith in Jesus as our Lord and Savior.

The verse I use to support this is from Ephesians 2:10, where it says, *For we are God's handiwork, created in Christ Jesus to do good works, which God prepared in advance for us to do.* There are two critical statements here, which we should believe and trust. The first is *we are all God's handiwork.* The second is that we are *created in Christ to do good works.*

These are critical statements to hold dear and close to our hearts. The first assertion of being *God's handiwork* is supported in Genesis 1:27, where it says, *So God created [human]kind in His own image, in the image of God He created them; male and female He created them*. Make no mistake about the fact that Jesus, through God, created us. And Jesus does not create inferiority. He created us in the image of God.

The second statement states that we were *created in Christ to do good works*. And we are! The key to our faith is believing Christ, and that includes the thought, *Christ created us to do good work*. All of us have this capacity and only have to believe in Jesus to fulfill this statement.

Jesus Loves Us

No matter what we think about ourselves, Jesus's love for us is biblical and genuine. In John 15:9, we get a complete view of Jesus's cycle of love, where Jesus says, *As the Father has loved Me, so have I loved you. Now remain in My love*. Notice how love flows from God to Jesus to us. But also notice Jesus's command at the end: *Now remain in My love*.

This also gets to our understanding of self-worth. We can either have too much self-worth or not enough. In both of these extreme cases, we are not finding our self-worth through Jesus but ourselves. The person who thinks too highly of themselves has put Jesus in the background and will eventually fall. The person with low self-worth has let others and not Jesus dictate their self-worth. Never let anyone but Jesus define you!

This is what Jesus is talking about in John 15:9; our focus should be on Him. Here's why: When we measure ourselves by what others think and what we think of ourselves, we subject ourselves to manipulation from others and ourselves. The input we receive about ourselves is not always mean-spirited manipulation. Sometimes it is just people telling us what we want to hear or people unloading their opinions about us because of their own issues. Jesus will never manipulate, falsely praise, or call us names.

No doubt, abusive personalities can do severe damage to our psyche. But we can also do the same damage to ourselves. When we fail, we get mad at ourselves, or we feel embarrassed. Then we start calling ourselves names. The last thing Jesus wants us to do is to call ourselves names, or for that matter, let others hurt our psyche. Instead, Jesus wants us to focus on doing better the next time and remember His love has only one condition: to have faith in Him as our Lord.

Jesus Makes Us Worthy

I have a good friend I wrote about in my last book, *Your Faith Has Made You Well.* She had an abusive stepmother who ridiculed her about her weight, leaving mental scars. As a result, she struggled with her unworthiness for years, only to escape to the Marines to hide. Then in her first marriage, she carried this unworthiness into that life. After extensive abuse by her husband, she finally divorced.

For years she struggled with, *Am I good enough?* Later, remembering the lessons of Jesus given to her by her grandmother, she began to recover her self-esteem. When she fully accepted Jesus in her life, she emerged as a powerful and confident businesswoman. She is now married to an extraordinarily devoted husband, with whom she runs a successful business.

As she stopped believing what others said about her and turned to Jesus, she found her real value. No longer does she measure herself against other people, and she is wary of what people say to or about her. Because of Jesus, she is strong!

Focus on Jesus

When we focus on ourselves and how other people treat us, we lose sight of Jesus. When others reject us, Jesus will still accept us. When Jesus says, *As the Father has loved Me, so have I loved you. Now remain in My love,* this isn't just *a nice thing to say* from

Jesus. It is a command to *remain in His love* and not let the fickleness of the world change the fact that you and we are all worthy because of our faith in Jesus.

We can also suffer from *impostor syndrome.* We don't believe that we are as good as we appear on the outside. When we fail, internally, we overstate our failures. We are sure we will be discovered as a fraud. We lose sight of the fact we are *made in the image of God.* We forget that all will fall short of perfection and that failing is part of the human condition.

We can also listen too much to criticism and not put as much weight on compliments. Trying to be balanced in what we hear is hard, and those with a propensity to self-deprecate tend to create false images of themselves. Jesus wants us to get our validation through abiding and remaining in His love. His love is the most authentic compass we have in this life.

There is a wonderful saying that goes like this: *It doesn't matter how many times you fall; it matters how many times you get up.* Failure is part of life. No one escapes making bad decisions or having shortcomings. With Jesus, it is not about our falling but our getting back up.

As Christians with faith, we are given this chance of getting back up and becoming better because of Jesus and His cross. Jesus wants us to forget our past and to focus on being better tomorrow. The very next step or action we take should be our best. Self-worth is rebuilt with the stringing together of Jesus, like activities that reinforce we are worthy.

Jesus wants us to focus on Him and His teachings; this is the true path to worthiness. We will always be deceived by what others and ourselves say about us. Focusing on the self and not Jesus is a dead-end street.

How do we rise above the voices and things we encounter that detract from our self-worth? We do this by measuring what we hear and see based on what we know about the Gospel. If it matches, then we can accept what we have seen and heard as real. Staying close to the Gospel and Jesus will create a healthy sense of self-worth.

Finding Self-Worth by Helping Others

Another way to rebuild our self-worth is through our service. When we adhere to the lesson of Jesus to *love our neighbor,* we begin to do things that help others. In this helping, our feeling of self-worth becomes enhanced, both in what we hear and how we feel about ourselves. And it also makes us feel more ethical in our actions, further enhancing our self-esteem.

What we find in our generosity is that it is no longer important what others say about us, but it allows us to acknowledge in ourselves that Jesus is correct. We are capable of good. We will begin to worry if we have done enough for Jesus. And here is the point: any action that helps our neighbor, Jesus will tell us it was good, and we will feel worthy.

I recently spoke to a senior person at a local food bank and asked him about this phenomenon. He completely agreed. What he sees in the volunteers is joy. The more they help, the more they want to help. It is like going to a spa and getting an elixir filled with self-worth.

Jesus also asks us to *love God.* When our actions show our love for God, we begin to do those things that please God. These actions are always right and reinforce that we are capable of doing good. Again the more actions we string together that show we love God, the more we feel self-worthy.

To Forgive Is Divine

Another aspect of feeling worthy is forgiveness: being able to forgive ourselves and others. If we are weak at forgiving ourselves, then likely we will also be weak in forgiving others. When we forgive others, we see their value. Likewise, when we forgive ourselves, we see our value.

A critical part of forgiveness is repentance. Repent in Greek means *to change*. Indeed, if we keep making the same mistake over and over, then forgiveness becomes hollow. Jesus has forgiven all our sins and likewise gives us a second chance to try a different way, to change the way we live. This process involves our heart. We don't simply change because we are requested to change. We change because our hearts want to change.

Many ask me, *Is a convict on death row worthy of Jesus's forgiveness?* My reply is yes! Again, so long as their acceptance of Jesus is faithful and true. This is a challenging message for many. They will say, *How could that be true, after all they have done?*

Part of being faithful is forgiving and realizing it is not our job to judge. Instead, it is Jesus's job to judge. Here's why: The minute we judge, we are assuming we have all the facts and thinking we truly know the other person's heart, both big and bold assumptions. When we judge, we set ourselves in the judgment seat in place of Jesus, which is always a perilous place to be mentally!

If we want to feel worthy, we have to be all in with forgiveness, especially if we want the same forgiveness.

I recently asked on Twitter, *What was the hardest thing about being faithful to Jesus and His teachings?* By far, the largest response was forgiveness and turning the other cheek. So, we aren't alone with this challenging assignment. But to feel worthy, we must *love our neighbor* unconditionally.

Part of making *Jesus our everything* is feeling worthy. Self-worth is not derived from what we hear said to us or what we say to ourselves. Instead, self-worth is derived by knowing we are *made in the image of God* and truly believing we are. And to know when Jesus said, *As the Father has loved Me, so have I loved you. Now remain in My love,* it is entirely and absolutely true!

Surely, in everyone's lives, we will encounter abusive personalities. We will certainly all have regretful actions at some point. And some will be too hard on themselves all the time.

Instead of letting these factors dictate how we feel about ourselves, know deeply and faithfully that Jesus loves us, so much so that He made that difficult walk to the cross for our redemption. When we cross this bridge of faith, we will be worthy, and Jesus will become *everything*.

6

Our Relationship with Jesus Is a Two-Way Street

*Here I am! I stand at the door and knock. If anyone hears
my voice and opens the door, I will come in and eat with
that person, and they with me.*

—Revelations 3:20

If we want Jesus to be everything, then
we have to involve Jesus in everything in our lives. Everything
we hope for and live for should be through Jesus. This extends
to our personal relationship with Jesus. The relationship
shouldn't be just when we need Jesus. It should always be a
continuous conversation that involves all the times of our lives.
We will sometimes catch ourselves only praying when we need
something, forgetting about the many blessings we have and
not thanking Jesus. In effect, we are simply seeking Jesus when
we need something, making Jesus just our genie.

Instead, we should become more balanced in the ways we
treat Jesus. It is always right to pray to Jesus for help in our
lives, but it is just as important to recognize the blessings of Jesus. In this way, we elevate Jesus from being our servant in
times of stress to being our Lord and benefactor.

Recently, on my Twitter feed, I received a message from a
follower who best describes this thought. They wrote, *He's the*

same to me every day. The one constant in my life that never changes. The perfect constant. The beacon of hope. I'll continue my walk with Christ to build my relationship with Him. He's always by my side to converse with day or night. It's a relationship, not a religion. For this person, Jesus is all he needs. He doesn't see Jesus as a genie but instead as a relationship to be developed and nurtured. And this is what Jesus wants from all of us: not to be a genie but to be with us every moment of our lives.

The Importance of Thankfulness

I have a good friend who does something each day that short circuits a one-sided relationship with Jesus. Each morning, as he says his prayers, he intentionally remembers the good things from the day before and thanks, Jesus. My friend says of this activity, *It opens my eyes with a greater sense of gratitude.*

I love this concept of remembering the blessings of the previous day and then thanking Jesus. This remembrance of the previous day's blessings reinforces the importance of Jesus in our lives. It also strengthens and reminds us that Jesus knows our heart's greatest desires. This thanking gives us time to reflect on how closely the blessings tie back to our prayers.

Now, I am not saying that we shouldn't ask for help from Jesus. Simply, I am saying any relationship needs to have gratitude and assistance to work. We all know those who only want to tell us about their problems or just call us when they need something. Try as hard as we might, after too many of these conversations, we lose interest.

Now Jesus will never lose interest in us, but our relationship with Jesus will be flawed because we fail to see the connection of Jesus's responses to our prayers and blessings. And failure to thank Jesus is a slippery path to compartmentalizing Jesus. We will never have a complete relationship without complete obedience to being thankful for Jesus's involvement in our lives.

Make no doubt about it, Jesus wants to be fully in our lives, not pushed over to a convenient time for us. Jesus wants to be with us and to hear all we have to say. Jesus wants to teach us, love us, guide us, and sanctify us. We only have to let Jesus in all the time, faithfully.

Jesus Is *Knocking* on Our Door

In the verse for this chapter, we find this mutual relationship that Jesus wants. In Revelations 3:20, it says, *Here I am! I stand at the door and knock. If anyone hears my voice and opens the door, I will come in and eat with that person, and they with me.*

As a side note, the verse says, *If anyone hears My voice and opens the door!* This means all are asked to answer. It is our answering that decides our status, in or out.

When you read this verse, you see this sense of mutuality, especially in the word *with.* From this verse, we can see that Jesus doesn't want a *command-and-control* relationship. Rather, Jesus wants to tell us about His dreams for us, and He wants to hear what we are hoping for. Jesus wants us to listen and understand His message.

What's important to remember in these conversations is that God is talking to us through Jesus. And when we either hear or read the Word of God, it is always authentic and pure. There is no manipulation or ulterior motive. It is the purest truth we will ever hear. So while we may view this as a mutual relationship (and it is), the sacredness of Jesus raises this conversation above a human relationship. It will become our most important life relationship: one that we can always count upon.

The next thing to take from this verse is Jesus's knocking. This knocking will never stop until we fully *open the door.* I call this the compelling force of Jesus. Jesus wants in and to be fully in. Sure, He could knock down the door and barge in, but what point would that serve? We don't listen to pushy people. Rather, Jesus, throughout our lives, will always compel us to talk *with* Him. We can push Jesus away or ignore the knock, but the knocking will never cease until we let Jesus in.

A story about John Wesley, the founder of Methodism, helps highlight this compelling nature of Jesus. As Wesley was spreading the message of Jesus throughout England in the eighteenth century, he gathered up a few of his new pastors and stated, *We must spread the word to Bristol.* Bristol was a town of ill repute in the eighteenth century, filled with schemers, thieves, and prostitutes—a difficult place to find good.

The pastors asked Wesley how they could bring Jesus to such a place. Wesley replied, *Jesus is already there waiting for us to help.* Jesus's compelling nature abounds everywhere and with every person, even in the darkest moments.

The Reluctant Convert: Augustine

For the great early church father Augustine, Jesus *knocked* hard and long. Especially in the form of his mother, Monica, who lovingly and persistently tried to get Augustine to open up to Jesus. Monica watched Augustine bumble through life disquieted until in a garden in Milan, he let Jesus in. Augustine's quote about this experience was very revealing, explaining when he fully accepted Jesus knocking, *his heart was quieted.*

Augustine went on from this point to dedicate his life to serving his Lord, ultimately becoming the Bishop of Alexandria and the early creator of many Christian practices and thoughts. After a life of struggling and not answering Jesus's knock, Augustine found his purpose.

Augustine was raised in North Africa by a modestly wealthy family. He was able to attend school and became a skilled writer. In his youth, he was in constant pursuit of the truth and prone to being mischievous. His mother Monica urged Augustine to seek Jesus to find the truth. The more Monica pushed him, the further away Augustine moved toward other avenues to find the truth of life.

He sought out any religious group or philosophy to find his answers, only to fall short or become disillusioned, seeing many of the various philosophies and leaders as flawed.

Augustine was also a party goer and enjoyed many late nights with his friends. He and his friends were quite popular on the social scene. Augustine's ability to speak fast and with wit made him a favorite with women. One of Augustine's most famous quotes is *Give me chastity, but not yet.* Two things kept Augustine from hearing Jesus knocking: his social life and his determination to find the truth independently.

After Augustine finished his studies, he was recognized as a skilled scholar and was invited to Milan to teach. His mother, who was concerned with her son, followed Augustine to Milan. As a devout Christ-follower, she met the Bishop of Milan, to whom she constantly appealed to Augustine to meet.

Finally, Augustine met his equal in oratory and had many conversations with the bishop. Over time, the bishop chiseled away at Augustine and his doubts about Jesus. Sitting in a garden in Milan in 386 AD, Augustine finally gave in and answered Jesus's *knocking.*

Putting the Ways of Jesus First

Not all of us will or have to follow the life that Augustine led to completely accepting Jesus's knock. Some might say, *How do I follow Jesus entirely and give up my career, family, and other aspects of my life?* The answer is you don't. Completely following Jesus simply means putting the ways of Jesus first. Living a productive life is not inconsistent with following Jesus. The Apostle Paul said, *There are different kinds of gifts, but the same Spirit distributes them. There are different kinds of service, but the same Lord. There are different kinds of working, but in all of them and in everyone it is the same God at work* (1 Cor. 12:4–6).

Notice Paul says *different kinds of* three times. As we have said before, whenever a phrase or verse is said three times in the Bible, it is important, symbolic of completeness. Paul's point is that we all have gifts, and following these gifts isn't inconsistent with completely giving ourselves to Jesus.

Especially as it relates to our work, not everyone has the gift of ministry. Some are given the gift of healing or perhaps the gift of counseling or business. Regardless of the gift that has been given to us by the Holy Spirit, Paul says, we have the *same Lord*. This is a crucial point in how we live and follow Jesus. We all have the *same Lord*.

So what does that mean? If you are a physician, give the patient the best service you can and treat the patient wisely as if working for the Lord. Or, if you are a counselor, serve your patients as if you serve the Lord. If you are a business person, simply treat your customers with fairness. Treat every person you deal with in your business life well. It also means do your best work all the time and without deception. No matter your occupation, simply work as if you are working for the Lord.

Jesus knows we have to work and wants us to be able to pay our bills. Jesus also wants us not to let money dictate our behavior and remember Him. When we answer the *knocking on the door*, we are adding to our lives and not sacrificing.

This doesn't mean we won't have to give things up or pay a price. We will. This will mean giving up those bad things for our health, perhaps being more generous with our money and spirit, and finally, devoting time to be with Jesus.

To have Jesus be everything means Jesus has to be fully let into our lives. Jesus isn't someone we call on only in times of stress. Jesus is a new way of life and far greater than just a helper. Jesus is the Lord and Savior. Jesus wants us to hear and answer His *knocking*. Even after we ignore the *knocking*, Jesus does not go away. When we answer, we will be surprised, amazed, and filled with the real truth. Our only hurdle is to make the step to answering the knocking on our door.

7

Surrendering Everything Makes Jesus Everything

Then Jesus said to his disciples, "Whoever wants to be my disciple must deny themselves and take up their cross and follow me. For whoever wants to save their life will lose it, but whoever loses their life for me will find it."

—Matthew 16:24–25

The simple truth of life is that everything we have and have done is through the grace bestowed upon us by Jesus. For some, this is a hard concept to accept fully. Crossing this barrier of understanding is difficult because of temptation, worry, and ego. It does not mean we have to give back everything God has freely given us. Rather, if required, we should be completely willing.

This is a hard battle to fight. We like what we have, and we can't possibly see how we can get along without it. It is not that Jesus wants to take it back. It is that Jesus wants us to be willing to give it back. Jesus will call upon us at various times in life to share our time, money, and our possessions. And this means getting off our current track and helping out.

Changing Our Course

I have a good friend, Geoff, who will always stop if he sees someone in distress. No matter his current path, he will always stop and find out how he can help. Recently, as we were walking back from a restaurant to our car, he noticed a man under a train trestle who seemed confused.

Geoff approached him cautiously and asked, *Are you okay?* The man replied, *I am.* This discourse went on for a few more moments with my friend making sure the man was okay. Geoff had changed his path for a few brief moments to help someone out. It is not a big surrendering; instead, it reflects how instinctively Geoff thinks of other people first.

A similar event occurred when Geoff, his wife, my wife Connie, and I were heading to the golf course. As we were driving, Connie and Geoff noticed a woman falling in the street.

Immediately they both asked for me to stop the car and pull over. Connie, an EMT, and Geoff jumped out of the car to tend to the woman. I got out and stopped the traffic until the ambulance arrived to assist the woman. The whole incident took no less than 15 minutes. Two earthly angels, Geoff and my wife, took on helping despite having a different destination.

This was a moment of giving up our intended path to help, a disruptive moment to aid a fellow human being in distress. This was a simple moment of surrendering to aid. These are the moments that Jesus wants us to pause our routines and take time to help out.

Gary: Jesus's Humble Servant

Another of my friends, Gary, has achieved substantially less than a person of his abilities or status should have received materially. Regardless, I think of him as a person filled with great spiritual bounty.

He is both humble and mild. When he talks with people, he listens for subtleties in an attempt to help. He is always looking for clues to assist. His responses are polite suggestions, not insistent or pushy. His demeanor is one of calmness and thoughtfulness. His number one goal is to leave the person better off and with something to ponder.

Gary is a pastor for a major national denomination. He has labored at small churches for years and was never assigned to a blossoming large church. He has always been looked over when these prestigious assignments have come up. Yet when you talk to him, that subject will not be brought up. He prefers to discuss how he can help.

Likewise, he is a qualified pharmacist. He doesn't work for a big firm. Instead, he runs a clinic to help those with addictions. He gets up early every day and greets the addicted at the clinic. He knows all about these people. He knows who is desperately seeking freedom from drugs and who is still in denial. He knows the manipulative behavior of those seized by the awful disease of addiction. He serves because he has found his Christian purpose, and it fills him with joy.

In my conversations with Gary, he was always the one asking questions, with me seeking answers. Any attempt on my part to turn this conversation in a different direction is always politely rebuffed. He surrenders his need for relevancy strictly to help me.

Gary was assigned to me as I was pursuing my ministerial calling and potentially becoming a minister. He probed to discover more and to see where Jesus was leading me. Gary noticed that I thought differently.

He watched as I got frustrated with the board that selects ministers. The more I tried to explain why I wanted to be a minister, the more tongue-tied I became. Gary sensed this and, at the same time, felt I was called to serve but differently. It wasn't that the review board was mistreating me. It was more that they sensed I hadn't fully captured my mission in service to Christ. They knew there was a calling, but not as an in-house pastor.

Gary saw this struggle and politely kept nudging me to think differently. For most seminary students, church ministry is a natural choice. Gary saw something different for my ministry. He gently guided me to think of an alternative ministry, which is what I do today: a nontraditional ministry of informing. He spent extra time with me, for which I was grateful. He nursed this direction humbly and purposefully.

When I think or speak of Gary, I know he has given up a lot to serve. He certainly could have been greater in wealth and status. His wealth is found in helping others. Long ago, he surrendered to Jesus and followed his current course. He serves the way Jesus wants him to serve, listening and taking care of all of us.

Serving Two Masters Is Impossible

Surrendering to Jesus also means forgoing that which tempts us in an unhealthy way. Many things tempt us: drugs, alcohol, and lust. These are the most obvious temptations and certainly have ensnared many. Many of us will look at those trapped with either empathy or sadness. These are the easy temptations to identify.

Beyond the obvious temptations lies an equally dangerous and more subtle temptation: a life in which we serve another master than Jesus. Perhaps it is the pursuit of money or fame, a place where we put the ways of the world ahead of Jesus.

Even if we don't have an outward addiction, that doesn't mean we aren't trapped in a life away from Jesus. This other life might be greatly approved of by those who surround us but can easily be as destructive to our being.

This approval we receive falsely empowers us to seek this other path. The gains we temporarily receive from this alternative life will push us further from the path of Jesus. Inevitably, because of the fickleness of this world, we will find ourselves at a place we didn't want to be.

A friend of mine, always a devout Christian, had started to rise up the ranks in his company. As he rose, the perks of the job began to give him the wealth he had never imagined. The higher up he went, the greater the earthly reward. Over time, the rewards started to occupy his thoughts completely. He began to stretch his values to ensure he met the goals set out for him. Soon he found himself in a place far removed from Jesus. Money occupied his thoughts and motives.

Jesus talks about this in Matthew 6:24, where He says, *No one can serve two masters. Either you will hate the one and love the other, or you will be devoted to the one and despise the other. You cannot serve both God and money.* As we chase the value of money, we become tempted to push away the importance of Jesus.

The irony here is that following Jesus's ways does not mean you won't still be successful in your career. My friend still would have been successful because he was a good employee. It was the lure of money that caused him to stretch further than he should, compromising his efforts, relationships and choices, just to get ahead. The subtlety is falsely thinking the extra we gain is real and worthwhile. Instead, it makes our efforts more erratic and more likely to create discord in our relationships and performance.

There is a fine line that has to be managed internally in our minds. It is either not trying to be successful or trying too hard to be successful. We are either letting our families and ourselves down by not being the best, or we reach beyond the point Jesus wants us to be. In Proverbs 30:8–9, we get a fantastic description of this state:

> Keep falsehood and lies far from me;
> > give me neither poverty nor riches,
> > but give me only my daily bread.

>Otherwise, I may have too much and disown You
> and say, "Who is the LORD?"
>Or I may become poor and steal,
> and so dishonor the name of my God.

Surrendering our lives to Jesus doesn't mean we will be poor. Surrendering our lives to Jesus means whatever we achieve will be honorable.

By Surrendering We Gain

Another friend who was successful in his career told me he never asked for a raise or extra perks. Instead, he sought out those companies and managers that held integrity and thoughtfulness as preeminent values. His focus was on finding the right spot to be able to succeed.

In one unusual case, when money was tight one year, he asked his employer to pass on him for a raise so others could receive more. Now on the surface, this might sound silly to some. In reality, it was a wise decision. His heart was pointed to service and not self-gain.

Later on, his company, which valued integrity and teamwork, promoted him. His goal wasn't to get promoted; instead, it helped those who would have had less.

This is the surrendering Jesus is talking about in Matthew 16:24–25, where Jesus says, *If anyone wishes to come after Me, he must deny himself, and take up his cross and follow Me. For whoever wishes to save his life will lose it; but whoever loses his life for My sake will find it (NASB 1995).* Jesus doesn't mean we literally will lose our lives. Jesus means we will find real life when we live for Jesus.

Surrendering everything to Jesus is not a giving up. It is a receiving activity. Ironically, the more we suppress ourselves to live life Jesus's way, the more we gain.

True joy doesn't come from the material things we acquire; rather, it comes from how we live. The surrendering doesn't mean we will have easy days, and no manner of living can ensure an easy life. Surrendering to Jesus means our difficult days will be addressed with sustainable actions, which produce a closer experience with Jesus. These steps both prepare us for the future and give us a life of greater certainty.

For Jesus to be our everything, we should surrender our wills to Him. It isn't as hard as we may think. The first step is the hardest; the rest are easier.

8

Choose Jesus; He Has Already Chosen You

You did not choose Me, but I chose you and appointed you so that you might go and bear fruit—fruit that will last—and so that whatever you ask in My name the Father will give you.

—John 15:16

For some Christians, praying and going to church on Sunday is the extent of their relationship with Jesus. Indeed, these are good practices. Some of us read the Bible daily, and that is also a good practice.

Jesus wants more. Jesus wants us to truly love Him: not just go to church, pray, or even read the Bible. Jesus wants us to choose Him in all that we do because He has chosen us. To do this, Jesus wants us to move from ritualistic practices that are passive to being actively involved with Him.

As Jesus was nearing the end of His earthly mission, He gathered the disciples together for one last pep talk. He began His address by discussing a grapevine. He said, *I am the true vine, and My Father is the gardener (John 15:1)*. Later in the talk, Jesus told the disciples, *You did not choose Me, but I chose you and appointed you so that you might go and bear fruit—fruit that will last—and so that whatever you ask in My name the Father will give you (John 15:16)*. In this message, Jesus told the disciples He *chose* them. He called out to them and compelled them to join Him on the vine of life.

Jesus also told them to *bear fruit, fruit that will last*. His selection of the disciples was due to His love for them. Accepting Jesus's choice carries a responsibility. Bearing fruit is an active expression of what Jesus wants. While Jesus wanted them to pray, have faith, and stay close to Him, He also wanted them to go out in the world and make it a better place.

Likewise, for us, Jesus chooses us because He loves us. While we may not be one of His original disciples, we are still part of Jesus's flock. He wants us to be part of *His vine*. This verse applies to those of us in the twenty-first century as strongly as it did to those from the first century. Remaining in Jesus means *bearing fruit*.

Agape Love

We may ask, *Is that all there is? And is it this simple?* The answer to these questions is yes, but it also means we must love Jesus with all our hearts and souls. We also need to understand the depth and meaning of this love.

His message of love is simple, and we find it in John 14:23, where it says, *Anyone who loves Me will obey My teaching. My Father will love them, and We will come to them and make our home with them.* This sounds easy: love Jesus, and God will love you, leading us to a place where we reside in the divine. Now the love Jesus is talking about is called, in Greek, *agape*. It means unconditional love: preferential love that is chosen and acted out by the will. It is not love based on goodness or upon natural emotion. Instead, this is benevolent love that always seeks good.

This love is a choice. When we love Jesus, we receive *agape* love that seeks to help us and is for our benefit. Let's be careful here: it doesn't mean we will always get what we want (that would be a disastrous form of love). Instead, this love is giving us all that we need.

Finally, Nicodemus *Bears Fruit*

Earlier in the Gospel of John, we meet Nicodemus, who is an excellent example of this calling from Jesus and moving to love Jesus. In John chapter three, we find Nicodemus seeking Jesus in the middle of the night. Fearful others would see him, Nicodemus approaches Jesus nervously.

Nicodemus was a powerful force in Jerusalem, a well-respected member of the ruling body called the Sanhedrin. In a worldly sense, it could be disastrous if he was found talking with Jesus. For the Sanhedrin, Jesus posed a threat because of His radical ideas. Jesus threatened their power base.

Despite this risk, Nicodemus felt strangely compelled to talk with Jesus. An inner voice had told him to discover more. In reality, Jesus had entered Nicodemus's heart.

Now Nicodemus was taking the step to discover more. This action compelled by Jesus would lead Nicodemus to begin the complicated process of giving up his life of luxury to obtain the gift of love from Jesus. Many long nights lay ahead for Nicodemus. He might have much to lose in worldly terms to gain Jesus.

This process began when Nicodemus asks Jesus, *Rabbi, we know that You are a teacher who has come from God. For no one could perform the signs You are doing if God were not with him (John 3:2).*

Jesus replies, *Very truly I tell you, no one can see the Kingdom of God unless they are born again (John 3:3).*

Then Nicodemus reveals his lack of understanding when he says, *How can someone be born when they are old? ... Surely they cannot enter a second time into their mother's womb to be born! (John 3:4)*

There it was; Nicodemus approached every part of his life with earthly logic. To Nicodemus, everything could be explained by what he knew and how things fit together. Nicode-mus became successful in the world by applying this earthly logic to all items. Reasoning centered around the world's ways was a significant hurdle for Nicodemus to really knowing and accepting that Jesus had chosen him.

He couldn't comprehend the divine. He lacked the type of faith that doesn't come from worldly logic. It is acquired through experience with Jesus and receiving grace. Faith comes from giving up a desire to be accepted by the world to accept-ing Jesus choosing us. To become part of Jesus's vine, Nicode-mus only had to have faith Jesus was who He said He was.

Nicodemus had a lot to give up if he followed Jesus. In a time and place where only a small percentage of the population lived with adequate resources and power, Nicodemus was very fortunate to have both. What prevented Nicodemus from grasping the message of Jesus was fear of losing power, respect, and an easy life.

Yet Nicodemus felt compelled to hear more and listen to Jesus. Jesus delivered a more comprehensive explanation by saying, *Very truly I tell you, no one can enter the Kingdom of God unless they are born of water and the Spirit. Flesh gives birth to flesh, but the Spirit gives birth to spirit. You should not be surprised at My saying, "You must be born again." The wind blows wherever it pleas-es. You hear its sound, but you cannot tell where it comes from or where it is going. So it is with everyone born of the Spirit (John 3:5–8).*

Jesus was talking about the *Holy Spirit* while Nicodemus was still using his human senses to sort things out about Jesus. This well-educated man was hung up on earthly things and needed more time to get comfortable with what he had to give up.

Over time, Nicodemus continued watching Jesus closely, still compelled to know more but always careful he didn't commit too quickly.

Later at a festival, Jesus created more believers. So much so, the leaders of the Sanhedrin and Pharisees desired to kill Jesus. Nicodemus came to Jesus's defense in a veiled way by saying, *Does our law condemn a man without first hearing him to find out what he has been doing? (John 7:51).*

When the other leaders listened to this, they asked Nicodemus to learn more, essentially delaying any action against Jesus. Nicodemus had given a half-hearted defense of Jesus while still moving down the road of understanding Jesus.

Nicodemus continued moving closer to fully accepting Jesus, but it was not until after the crucifixion that he fully came out of the closet and supported Jesus along with his friend, Joseph of Arimathea.

Nicodemus provided him with a burial spot and the spices to prepare His body for burial. In fact, Nicodemus bought 75 pounds of spices to accomplish this task, costing him a large amount of money. Jesus was given a burial only the elite would receive. Nicodemus was now entirely in and had accepted Jesus's choosing.

Now we can all say it took too long for Nicodemus to get and accept the message of Jesus, but are we any different? Especially those with a lot to lose when they truly choose Jesus and His way. For Nicodemus, it meant he might have to sacrifice his standing in society and his trained logical thinking. Nicodemus had to choose between the *Spirit of the Divine* and his earthly knowledge to fully understand why Jesus chose him.

The Woman at the Well

Later in the Gospel of John, we discover a different person whom Jesus calls upon, a woman with nothing to lose. At noon, a Samaritan woman went to her local well, Jacob's well, to draw water for the day. Jesus was alone and already there. As the woman began drawing water, Jesus said to her, *Will you give Me a drink? (John 4:7).*

The Samaritan woman responded, *You are a Jew and I am a Samaritan woman. How can you ask me for a drink? (John 4:9).* In other words, *Why have you chosen me?*

Jesus ignored her response and got to the point He wanted to discuss by saying, *If you knew the gift of God and who it is that asks you for a drink, you would have asked Him and He would have given you living water (John 4:10).*

Before we go any further, we need to examine the woman and who she was. Like most verses in the Bible, there is a lot hidden just below the surface. First, why would a woman in the Middle East be at the well drawing water for the day in the heat of the day? Why does it matter that she was a Samaritan woman? And we should know in the first century, it was highly irregular that a woman would speak to a man alone.

The answers to these points all lead to what a person from the first century would already know. Those of us from the twenty-first century would miss these points. First, she was likely an outcast from her society. We know this because she didn't draw her daily water from the well with her community's other women. They would go early in the morning to draw water for the day. Going during the heat of the day in the Middle East was not practical. Likely, she was an outcast and not accepted by those in her community.

The second interesting aspect is she was a Samaritan. The local Jewish population considered Samaritans inferior, and it was against local customs for there to be conversations between the Jewish and Samaritan people.

This separation goes back many centuries after King Solomon's death when the remnants of the original 12 tribes of Israel decided to split up. Principally, the existing Jewish population was made up of the Tribe of Judah while the Samaritans were the remainder. Over the previous centuries, hostility built up, leading to this awkward relationship between these groups.

In this woman, we have three significant clues about her lowly status. She was an outcast from her community. She was also an outcast from the larger society because she was a Samaritan. And finally, in the first century, women had very little say over their lives and were just a step up from being a slave. She was remarkably low on the socioeconomic scale.

This is what makes this story interesting. A woman who was quite different from Nicodemus, she had nothing to lose and was chosen by Jesus. Jesus used water as their conversation piece to let her know what Jesus wanted to talk about. Her barrier to accepting Jesus isn't status or material possessions; she has neither. Her barrier was, *Why did you choose me?*

She probed Jesus about His order of lineage in Jewish history, which Jesus ignored. Instead, Jesus tells her that He knew she had had a difficult life with five husbands and the one she was living with wasn't her husband (scandalous behavior in any century). After Jesus told her He knew everything, she exclaimed, *I know that Messiah (called Christ) is coming. When He comes, He will explain everything to us (John 4:25).*

Jesus declared, *I, the One speaking to you—I am He (John 4:26).* Again there is a subtle clue. When Jesus said, *I am He,* He was referring to himself as God. Whenever we see the expression, *I Am* in the Bible, it is God talking.

After this, she was satisfied that Jesus was God and God was talking with her. His supernatural explanation of the circumstances of her life convinced her as well as the statement, *I am He.*

She then left to get her neighbors and community to talk with Jesus. Seeing her passion, her community's leaders invited Jesus to stay with them for a few days. After they spent time with Jesus, they also believed Jesus was divine and the long-awaited Messiah.

This lowly woman was responsible for the first evangelically large conversion in the Gospels. Jesus chose her even though she had led a tough life. Jesus saw her passion for finding out more and knew she would spread His message, something others might not have seen.

Jesus chooses all, even the lowest of society. Jesus doesn't worry about status, questionable pasts, gender, or worth. He wants all part to be of *His vine*. This story, contrasted with the Nicodemus story, demonstrates that Jesus will meet us where we are so that we can experience Him and His love.

When Jesus calls and chooses us, it requires us to think differently to accept this choice. Indeed, it will require a deeper conversation with Jesus, as it was with Nicodemus and the woman at the well.

To accept Jesus's choice also means we are willing to *bear fruit*. For Nicodemus, it meant taking a controversial stand of supporting Jesus in the dark hours of the crucifixion. It meant rising up for the woman at the well despite her lowly status in helping convince an entire community to find Jesus.

Wrestling with Jesus

Even today, there are stories and wonderful examples of people accepting Jesus's love and accepting Jesus's choice of us being part of *His vine*, modern twenty-first-century people who answered Jesus's compelling call.

I met John at a book signing for my book *Jesus & Co.* He is the pastor of a small church in rural North Carolina. As the afternoon wore on, he drifted over to the table, looked at my book, and then wandered away. After a few of these short visits, I sensed that he wanted to say more, so I asked a few questions.

He told me about his current life as a pastor and believer, but he also revealed a deeper story. John talked about the many nights when he had wrestled with Jesus. He described it as a mighty fight. He had been prone to staying out late and drinking, which affected his work and his family.

John persisted in following this twisted river in his life, despite its damaging effect. He knew it was wrong, but he did not feel he could change. He would try, only to slip back into what he perceived to be a place of comfort.

The inevitable moment came when he was stripped bare. His drinking and partying cost him his job, and he became utterly alienated from his family.

He had reached his tipping point, and his path had left him broken and alone. His comfortable habit of going out with the boys for long hours, which had affirmed his existence for years, had now left him no place but desolation.

Over the previous few months, he had been getting hints to change. Silently he had begun to question if he was on the right path. His discourse with Jesus had begun, but there was still too much to let go of in his current life to choose Jesus.

He liked the familiar path, so he wrestled with Jesus and resisted. Then the day came when it all came crashing in, and he was in a spot where he was so low he could only go up.

At first, John began to read the Bible, and through this reading, he set his course to a different path, one of accepting Jesus. Over time, this extended to his seeking to get an education and to become a pastor, both of which he accomplished.

I met him in a bookstore, with a devoted wife and a life he was proud of. He simply wanted to share. I saw, within both him and his wife, faithful love for Jesus. By wrestling with Jesus and losing, John had been healed. Jesus had chosen him, and he had finally relented.

He had been blind, but now he saw, and what he saw was a future that only contained a life filled with grace. He had been trapped, not because he was bad but because he followed a path built on destructive habits, a familiar course, even though it was disastrous.

He had given in to his natural human tendencies to pursue this life in which he found satisfaction, even though it was only momentary. John wanted to do good, but he believed he would not find comfort anywhere else. The Apostle Paul in Romans 7:15 says, *I do not understand my own actions. For I do not do what I want, but I do the very thing I hate (ESV)*. Even the great Apostle Paul struggled with this path and his natural desires.

So it is always with our faith. It is a struggle to avoid doing what we should not do, to turn away from the wrong path and move toward the right direction. For some, this may be easy, but for most, it is a hard lesson to learn that many times the wrong and destructive path we choose only reveals itself at the end.

While Jesus chooses all, not all immediately accept this choice. Some wait a lifetime. Others find Jesus through a crisis. Some never accept Jesus's choice.

Whether we are a rich man from the first century, a down-trodden person, or even a person who squandered his life, Jesus still chooses us. Jesus loves us. For this gift, we only need to have faith in the risen Christ and actively join His vine.

9

To Fully Experience Jesus, We Have to Imitate Jesus

*Do nothing out of selfish ambition or vain conceit.
Rather, in humility value others above yourselves, not
looking to your own interests but each of you to the
interests of the others. In your relationships with one
another, have the same mindset as Christ Jesus:*

—Philippians 2:3–5

There is an old saying that goes like this: *You are what your record says you are.* When I was a CFO for Fortune 500 companies, I would make this go-to comment when I sensed people were just going through the motions—speaking about what they wanted to accomplish without putting any substantial energy into their efforts. The same is true with our relationship with Jesus. To fully experience Jesus, we have to pitch in and live the Gospel, not just say the Gospel. In doing so, we imitate Jesus.

In imitating Jesus in our lives, we are also incarnating Jesus, making Jesus alive and doing His work. This is what Jesus asks of us. Simply knowing Jesus isn't enough. This knowledge needs to be shown in our tangible output. In the previous chapter, we talked about *bearing fruit* as part of our Christian life. Imitating Jesus is how we accomplish this effort.

The irony here is the more we do and act like Jesus, the more joy we find in our lives. We have all heard the phrase, *the more you give, the more you receive.* The statement applies broadly in our work for Jesus. Not that our intent should be to get more when we offer more. Rather our objective is to serve Jesus and humankind, which in turn strengthens our relationship with Jesus.

Imitating Jesus Isn't Radical

In 1942, Clarence Jordan and his wife, Florence, moved to a 400-acre farm in Americus, Georgia. Clarence had just received his Ph.D. from Southern Baptist Theological Seminary and finished four years as a missionary. They called their farm Koinonia, the Greek word meaning *fellowship,* a name they used to identify their purpose and one that is strongly connected to the first Christians portrayed in the Books of Acts. It was a Christian commune committed to sharing their resources and money.

To sustain their farm and community, they began growing peanuts. Interestingly, Clarence also had a degree in agriculture. This knowledge proved to be valuable in creating an economically sustainable community.

But Clarence did something very different than prevailing societal norms. He hired and recruited both black and white sharecroppers to help maintain and live on the farm.

He took vastly underpaid sharecroppers and gave them a chance to earn a living wage for their efforts. Clarence had long been troubled by his region's racial and economic injustice, making him desire to help these people in his community.

Well, this led to a substantial amount of backlash, and Koinonia became viewed as a considerable threat by the leaders in his community. There were bombings and boycotts, and Clarence himself was dismissed as a Southern Baptist minister.

The FBI investigated the farm as a communist stronghold. For a few years, life was tough for those living on the farm. Always resourceful, Clarence figured out a clever way to work around the boycott. The farm shipped their peanuts to other parts of the country and used the slogan *help us ship the nuts out of Georgia.* And it worked. The farm stayed self-sufficient.

An exciting turn in both Koinonia and Clarence's vision occurred in 1965. Millard and Linda Fuller visited the farm, intending to only stay for a few hours; instead, they moved onto the farm. By the age of 29, Milliard had become a self-made millionaire and was looking for a different path in life, and he found it at Koinonia.

The Fullers brought new energy to the farm and created a home-building initiative for those who could not afford new housing. After getting this initiative started and sustainable, the Fullers wanted to take what they had learned to Africa. And so they did. They went to the Democratic Republic of Congo and successfully started a similar home-building initiative. There they learned more methods of helping people have safe, sanitary, and secure housing.

During the Fullers time away, Clarence died in 1969. He was buried in an unmarked grave on the farm. But his legacy and methods continued. Leading one resident to say, *He be gone now, but his footprint is still here.*

Millard and Linda returned to the farm in 1976, armed with what they learned overseas and seeing the work they had started earlier on the farm of building homes was still growing. They decided to set up a new international organization to expand what they had learned and started.

This new organization snowballed throughout the United States and internationally. Today this organization still exists. Over the last 50 years, the organization has built over one million homes and helped well over ten million people, all from the vision of one man and other loyal Christians. Recently they built a new headquarters in Americus, Georgia, in honor of Clarence Jordan.

The name of this organization is Habitat for Humanity. Surprised? Well, many think this was Jimmy Carter's idea. It wasn't. Jimmy and his wife, Rosalyn, became great ambassadors for Habitat and helped make it a much larger organization. The idea came from the Fullers and Clarence.

On a side note, readers may remember the name Hamilton Jordan. He was Jimmy Carter's chief of staff during his presidency and the son of Clarence Jordan.

Many deserve a lot of credit for Habitat for Humanity. It was Clarence Jordan who created the right environment. His commitment to Christian values led to the rise of one of the world's most recognizable organizations.

When Clarence started Koinonia Farms, he believed the cause of poverty was spiritual and economic injustice. His life goal was to create a way to solve both, explaining why he was a scientifically trained farmer and held a doctorate in theology. Clarence had a simple plan: to help the sharecroppers of Georgia by imitating Jesus.

He brought the lessons of Jesus to life amidst the rural South's poverty and racism—a unique way to bring the Gospel's lessons into real-world practice. It reminds me of one of my favorite verses in the Gospels, from John 1:14, which says, *The Word became flesh and made His dwelling among us. We have seen His glory, the glory of the one and only Son, who came from the Father, full of grace and truth.*

And that's what Clarence did. He brought *Jesus the Word* to life in rural Georgia, not just because he was the guiding light of Habitat for Humanity, but he also radically changed the poor rural sharecropper's life in the South.

Clarence saw life through Jesus's eyes and imitated Jesus in every aspect of his life. He had no earthly model to follow but the example in Acts, in which early Christians lived in fellowship, tending to the poor spiritually and economically.

To the citizens of the nearby towns, his supposed radical approach was threatening. So radical the FBI investigated and looked for dangerous societal practices, when any of them could have just read the first few chapters of Acts to see where the idea came from.

No, Clarence's vision of bringing Jesus's lessons to life wasn't radical or subversive. It was simply one man carrying the message of the Gospels back to earth. What was revolutionary was Clarence's complete commitment to bringing the words of Jesus to life and sacrificing his wealth to help others.

Today, I read Clarence Jordan's sermons to give me ideas and learn his writing style. Through his writings (even after his death), this wonderful man who preached the Gospel when and wherever he could (from small churches to meeting houses, conventions, and large gatherings) continues to bring Jesus to life. I believe Clarence's words when I read them, not because of what he said but what he did.

Ordinary People Can Imitate Jesus

Not all of us will be great leaders of ministry, and that is the way God made life. For instance, only one of the original 12 tribes of Israel was slotted to become clergy-the Levites. The others were farmers, craftspeople, shepherds, and other needed occupations to maintain life in ancient times. Being a minister isn't the only way to imitate Jesus.

We will not all become Billy Graham, Martin Luther King, or Pope Francis. Ours is to lead a Christian life, which creates the bedrock of our faith. Our service to the Lord comes in everyday life. Our following of and imitating Jesus is our ministry. It is what the Holy Spirit assigns to us. Our work is equally as worthy when it is done in imitation of Jesus.

I have a friend, Mead, who, for me, best represents this everyday life. Mead has three children, a lovely wife, and works for a large bank. His every action throughout the day is a reflection of Jesus. Mead goes to church. He is a devoted father and husband. He is loyal and honest toward his customers. All that he says is designed to uplift.

His company provides a few days a year for the employees to help out in their community. Mead always participates and donates his time.

Mead gives to his church. He listens closely to his friends when they need helpful advice. He always provides his customers what they need and at no time compromises for his gain. He helps out with his children without being asked, and his favorite activity is working around the house. He is the son every mother wants. He is the father and husband that ministers talk about when discussing family affairs.

Now Mead's life might sound boring. And Mead will never be famous. This might be the only time you hear about him. He is another one of Jesus's *sled dogs* who creates the fabric of Christian life. Perhaps someday he will become famous and well known. It is unlikely. He doesn't seek fame. He seeks to be the best Christian.

He doesn't give to charity just to be seen. Nor does he serve to be noticed. He is the person Jesus describes in the Sermon on the Mount: people who don't pray to be seen.

For most of us, this is how our lives unfurl. Our reward isn't in being noticed by the world but by Jesus. The measure of who we are isn't to be judged by the world, but what Jesus sees us doing when no one is looking.

Unusual Ways of Imitating Jesus

Likewise, I have a friend, who we will call Bill. He competed for a sale to a large company and noticed his competitor had read the instructions wrong, creating a scenario in which he would win the deal through a fluke. Bill prayed about this and felt the Holy Spirit telling him to be fair to his competitor and point out his mistake. Bill did. Many might question this behavior on

Bill's part and say it is perfectly acceptable for him not to tell his competitor they made a mistake. This didn't sit right with Bill, so he told his competitor.

Interestingly, Bill still did win the contract. More importantly, he created goodwill with his competitor and the company. Many might say, *Why would he do that? His competitor wouldn't have.* This is the point: Jesus doesn't want our behavior dictated by how others treat us. Instead, it should be based on how Jesus wants us to treat our neighbor. This is another way we imitate Jesus.

When I was younger, starting a family and beginning to have success in my career, I began getting transferred to different parts of the country. With each move, a new church needed to be found. In a reasonably wealthy town in New Jersey, we found a new church. It was perfect. We loved the minister, the children's programs, and especially our small Bible study group.

A few months in, I had been spotted as a potential leader in the church and welcomed the opportunity. A few of the other committee chairs pulled me aside one Sunday to discuss the church organ. They wanted to move the organ around a little, so the organist could see the congregation without using a mirror—a small but expensive change.

I inquired about the cost and was told the whole project would be roughly $100,000. Previously, I heard about a church in a nearby community that had a fire, causing the church to close until they could fund the repair. Coincidently, the cost to repair this church was about the cost to slightly move the organ.

Innocently, I suggested giving the organ money to the church with the fire damage. I thought this was a normal and good suggestion. Those asking did not. What I said disappointed them. The minister had asked them to talk with me because of my financial background. Eventually, the organ did get moved, and the other church didn't get repaired.

To me, it seemed like the obvious answer was to help the fire-damaged church. If I could imagine Jesus being in charge, I believe He would have chosen to rebuild the church.

I tell this story about doing what Jesus would do to explain what imitating Jesus looks like. Sometimes we believe anything we do connected with the church is good. Many times this is true, so long as it honors and imitates Jesus as the incarnate God.

Jesus came to us to live with us. Our temples or churches don't exist to pay homage to Jesus by being just perfect. Instead, they are assembling points where the body (people) can meet. When we spend the church's money to make them prettier or just right, we ignore that Jesus is very present and God incarnate.

More simply, we forget to ask what Jesus would want us to do. When we ask this question and bring Jesus into our decision, Jesus becomes what He desires to be: present in our lives. Rebuilding another church would have been imitating Jesus.

Our goal in life should be to imitate what Jesus would do in all situations, not to gain fame. I am sure when Clarence Jordan set out, he didn't seek fame. He sought to help out the people who needed help. Clarence had the resources and the great gift of oratory. He used these gifts well. His main goal in life was to imitate Jesus and bring Him to life through his life.

Likewise, we also have gifts given to us by the Holy Spirit, and we should use them well. Most of us will never be famous, but those who serve will be just as important to Jesus. Most of us will be like Mead or Bill, not seeking fame, just serving the Lord.

When we imitate Jesus, we experience Jesus. In turns, this effort of experiencing builds our faith and pushes us deeper into making Jesus everything in our lives.

10

Don't Stay Trapped in the Past; Seek a Future with Jesus

Therefore, if anyone is in Christ, the new creation has come: The old has gone, the new is here!

—2 Corinthians 5:17

In 2 Corinthians 5:17, we read, *Therefore, if* *anyone is in Christ, the new creation has come: The old has gone, the new is here!* For some, I bet this is their most challenging concept in following Jesus. They let their past bind them in a sea of remorse. They are focusing on what they should have done and regretting past behaviors, mostly overstating the reality of their previous moments of failure.

To truly follow Jesus, we must believe these words from 2 Corinthians. Yes, we are new creations through Jesus. Each of us has stumbled. Everyone! Some of us may still be paying a steep price for our past. But know this: When we have faith in Jesus, He is no longer interested in our past. Jesus is interested in where we are going. The past is done, and the future is where Jesus wants us focused. Through the cross, we inherit freedom from our past. Believing this is an essential step in becoming a new creation and having a different future.

In a world where one slight misstep can get an individual *canceled,* redemption has become even harder to understand. The world will always try to drag us back into our dark moments and try to define us based on these events while at the same time ignoring our inherent good. This is the reality of the modern world, a fickle and agenda-ridden place. With Jesus, who we are is measured with real truth.

Jesus Operates Out of Love, Not Memory

Consider the woman Jesus saved from stoning. We read about this story in John 8:1–11. Jesus was confronted by the teachers of the law and the Pharisees, who attempted to trap and discredit Him. They brought forward a woman who had committed adultery and asked Jesus if it was okay to stone her according to the law of Moses. For Jesus, these learned men were missing the point. Jesus also knew answering this question was a trap to discredit Him. As Jesus did when He was being trapped by these types of malicious questions, He ignored their question.

Jesus bent down and started writing in the ground with His finger. Impatiently, the Pharisees and teachers asked Him what He was doing. Again Jesus ignored their question and said to them, *Let any one of you who is without sin be the first to throw a stone at her (John 8:7).* Slowly, from oldest to youngest, the crowd melted away until only Jesus and the woman were left.

Jesus stood up and looked at the woman and said, *Woman, where are they? Has no one condemned you?*

She replied, *No one, sir.*

In turn, Jesus said, *Then neither do I condemn you. Go now and leave your life of sin (John 8:10-11).*

Jesus knew of her past and did not punish her; instead, He commanded her to lead an unblemished life. Jesus is clearly more concerned with her future than her past, as He is with us. Where we have been isn't as important to Jesus as to where we are going.

In this story, the religious elite tried to trap Jesus by using a bystander and to potentially have her killed. They were more interested in getting Jesus trapped in a theological argument than the health and safety of a bystander. That is pretty callous stuff, I would say.

Because they had the power to prove a point, they tried to take advantage of a person who Jesus proved was no worse than themselves. This message is also important for us: Do not let the world judge you. Some people tied to worldly ways will trap us into thinking badly about ourselves to gain an advantage. Likewise, we should be cautious in how we judge.

While the world, other people, and even ourselves will try to keep us mired in issues from the past, Jesus has moved on. Jesus operates out of love, not memory. We have all failed, but the failures shouldn't define us. Rather, our capacity to love and do good is what defines us as worthy in Jesus's eyes.

Through the Cross, We Were Forgiven!

Always remember, Jesus's forgiveness for our sins was done on the cross. Jesus asks only two things: faith in Him and to *sin no more.*

In another story in Luke 7:36–50, we find Jesus at a Pharisee's house to have dinner. A woman who has lived a sinful life hears that Jesus will be at the Pharisee's home. She goes to the house uninvited. After entering the house, she immediately walked over to Jesus and started to sob. She knew who He was and the gift of forgiveness He brings. Unable to fully express her thankfulness, she kneeled on the floor and wiped Jesus's feet with her hair, moistened by the tears from her eyes. Then remarkably, this woman of little resources, with the expensive perfume she brought, anointed His feet.

One of the most powerful ways to honor a person in the first century was to wash their feet. Without the advantage of modern socks and shoes, feet could become very dirty from only walking with sandals. They would become rough and calloused. Washing someone's feet was a meaningful way to show respect and honor.

The Pharisee saw this and judged Jesus as not really a great religious man. Thinking to himself, *If this man were a prophet, He would know who is touching him and what kind of woman she is—that she is a sinner (Luke 7:39).*

Jesus knew what the man was thinking. He began to tell him a story and asked a question by saying, *Two people owed money to a certain moneylender. One owed him five hundred denarii, and the other fifty. Neither of them had the money to pay him back, so he forgave the debts of both. Now which of them will love him more?*

The Pharisee meekly replied, *I suppose the one who had the bigger debt forgiven.*

Jesus replied, *You have answered correctly (Luke 7:41-43).*

As the woman was leaving, Jesus said to her, *Your sins are forgiven (Luke 7:48).* Upon hearing this, the other guests questioned why Jesus forgave the woman.

Ignoring the guests, Jesus made one final and revealing statement to the woman: *Your faith has saved you; go in peace (Luke 7:50).* Her faith that Jesus was the Lord had saved her from her past, as it does with us. Jesus knew of her sin but also saw a changed heart.

When we look at this story from Jesus's point of view, we notice differing behaviors and contrasts. On the one hand, the most gracious of the people in the house was not invited and considered by the other guests as the most sinful. The Pharisee acted suspiciously of Jesus and even judged Him as an inferior religious person. The other guests questioned Jesus's authority. None but the sinful woman knew who Jesus was—the Lord.

So for the reader, who is the person in this story you admire? The ones who were judgmental or the one who was gracious and giving. Understanding this story helps us understand what Jesus is looking for. Jesus is looking for the person who, while flawed, is loving and generous. Jesus is also looking for one who has faith.

The woman did have a life of sin. She also was fervently seeking Jesus. She took the bold step of entering a home where she was uninvited and immediately went over to Jesus sobbing. Desperate to end her cycle of sin, she knelt, washed Jesus's feet, and then anointed them with expensive perfume. She was generous with her gift for Jesus and expressed her faith. Despite her past, she was a person Jesus was looking for.

The Pharisee was very different. He was intrigued by Jesus and invited Him for dinner. But his interest in Jesus wasn't sincere. At best, he saw Jesus as an equal: someone to know and potentially use as a resource in the future. The minute Jesus went outside of the social norm, by not rejecting the sinful woman, he thought lesser of Jesus. Jesus did not fit his image of what a *holy* person should look like, and he rejected Jesus.

Even the other guests at the party questioned Jesus and His actions, unsure how He could forgive the woman's sins.

Jesus isn't looking for people who conform to the ways of the world. Instead, Jesus is looking for people who in the future will be part of the Kingdom of God. Our past doesn't define us; our heart for Jesus defines us. We shouldn't stay mired in the past.

Jesus is clear in these two stories from the Gospel. He isn't interested in how well we conform to the world. Our pasts don't bother Jesus. It is our faith and hearts that Jesus seeks. When we put our faith in Jesus, we freely receive His *grace* and *mercy*.

Every person has something in their lives they regret, maybe many things. The two women's pasts in these stories are not much different than the people who tried to judge them. Their difference is the two women sought Jesus and heard His words, not the words of those who judged them.

One of our great sins is to stay handcuffed to our past, through what others say about us or even what we say about ourselves. Our faith in Jesus changes all of this. When we reach fervently out to Jesus, He will always tell us, *Go in peace and sin no more.* Believing this through our faith in Jesus releases us. We become *new creations,* and we make Jesus everything in our lives.

11

When You Help Jesus, Think Big!

Now to Him who is able to do immeasurably more than all we ask or imagine, according to His power that is at work within us.

—Ephesians 3:20

Tricia was homebound and isolated during the great pandemic of 2020. Her joy of helping others had been taken away from her. Mentally she was sinking, and she knew it. Every effort of her day was labored, and the effects of depression were setting in. Usually a vibrant woman who sought to help all she could, this gift was being taken from her.

Her pastor talked with her to lift her spirits and give her hope. He had sensed this weariness in her. Intently, he searched his mind to come up with a way to harness her spiritual energy, which would lift her out of the doldrums. He was watching a vibrant woman sink. This woman of God needed a new way to live life.

He saw the effect the isolation was having on others. Many of his programs to help the homeless and shut-ins were stopped because of the great pandemic. He knew Tricia should seek a new path and asked her for ideas.

Almost immediately, life poured back into her. Purpose replaced isolation. She had been a critical contributor to the feeding program her church had started a few months ago. With the pandemic, she knew the problem: people could no longer feel safe or be safe working together. Making meals together was unsafe.

As Tricia's pastor talked with her and through prayer, an idea popped up. She discovered she could still do the work of feeding. As she thought through the problem, she no longer felt depressing isolation. Her mind worked feverishly, and the time that previously labored her days became scarce.

It was simple: instead of cooking as a group, they could cook separately. When finished, they could take the meals to the church by themselves, making the church a central distribution point. Then individuals could pick up the meals and deliver them to those in need safely. The pastor agreed with the plan, and it was set in motion.

Tricia cooked the meals, at first just a few. Then she figured out that she could cook in larger quantities and break the larger amounts into smaller portions. It also reduced costs. At the same time, the pastor altered the delivery schedules and expanded the distribution.

Soon Tricia and her group were making 500 meals a week. She was now busier than she had been before the pandemic. She felt more joyous than even before she became a shut-in.

As she was thinking and organizing this new approach, she was constantly in prayer, asking Jesus to let her help. Her pastor asked her to accomplish something big with Jesus.

She gave up worrying about the resources. Other people came to provide what was scarce. Instead of life being limited, through service, life became boundless. Her lesson was to trust Jesus and plan big. Not to worry, but to do something, knowing half the effort was in starting.

When you work for Jesus, there are no limits. Jesus will also send us to a place just beyond our perceived abilities. We should remember any task Jesus gives us. He also provides the resources. You will know you are on the right path because difficult tasks will not be burdens. Instead, they will be joyous.

Jesus Rewards Faith

Thinking big with Jesus requires a courageous faith. While some may call this *blind faith,* it is not blind. It is a conscious act of obedience accompanied by butterflies in our stomach, a tension caused by a fear of failure. We might even say to ourselves, *How can I possibly do this?* A courageous faith overcomes these natural fears.

When I left the corporate world to enter theological school, at first, I was eager and optimistic that I would be a raving success. After I got accepted, I was confident and ready to go.

Then I got the notice. I needed to take a writing test to be appropriately placed in my first-year classes. At that moment, I gulped, and then reality hit me: *I am a terrible writer.* To pass a master's program English exam seemed impossible.

Thirty-five years earlier in my undergraduate studies, I had flunked English and had to go to summer school to make up the class. While I was successful in my business career, I always had a person who would work with me to handle the writing. This lack of writing further reduced my writing skills.

Soon I was sitting nervously at a desk, positive I would fail my writing exam, delaying my entry into my course work. After I prayed, I remember telling myself to just do my best and things will work out. I calmed my nerves, and I took the test. Surprisingly, I passed! I'm not sure how.

As I started my studies, I quickly learned why passing the writing test was necessary. In any given week, I was assigned hundreds of pages to read and to write the equivalent of a book or two during a semester. English and writing became my life.

At first, I stumbled around but finally realized I needed help or I would drown. I am not sure why, but I went to the school's theological librarian, Ernie.

Graciously he offered to help. And for the first few months, Ernie would review my writing. In the beginning, it would take me six hours to write a simple two-page assignment. The first semester was long and tiring. Thankfully, Ernie's cheery disposition kept me sane.

Without my realizing it, Jesus had placed me in an uncomfortable place educationally, having to make reading and writing my biggest asset. I was at a significant disadvantage. But Jesus didn't send me to this place in life without resources. Jesus also gave me a friendly librarian and professors who showed patience with my writing and graciously helped mold my grand ideas.

Remarkably, after seven years of working on a master's degree in divinity and a doctorate in ministry, I graduated with the honor of being the Daniel B. Kidder Award winner in Pastoral Theology for having the highest GPA. I hadn't set out to achieve this award. I had set out to survive. I had spent many hours writing and rewriting, long hours often filled with doubt. Every time I was ready to give up, I was bolstered by an unusual twist that would spur me on. I obeyed, and Jesus rewarded me.

I am still not a great writer. Instead, I have found great editors and resources that allow me to put on paper what the Lord wants me to say.

Jesus's Mom Thought Big!

For me, the story of Mary, Jesus's mother, is another example of thinking big. Imagine being a teenager and being approached by an angel who tells you that you will bear the Son of God.

It must have been a startling and challenging moment. Imagine you are engaged to be married and have come from a humble background in a backwater town of Judea. There would be nothing to prepare you for this task, and the risk would be high. As a woman who was engaged, becoming pregnant outside your marriage threatened social isolation plus a life of poverty. You would have no future. Yet Mary complied.

God sent the angel Gabriel to talk with Mary. Gabriel said to Mary, *Greetings, you who are highly favored! The Lord is with you (Luke 1:28).*

Mary became alarmed and wondered who this was and why they were so bold in their greeting.

Sensing her concern, Gabriel said, *Do not be afraid, Mary; you have found favor with God. You will conceive and give birth to a son, and you are to call Him Jesus. He will be great and will be called the Son of the Most High. The Lord God will give Him the throne of His father David, and He will reign over Jacob's descendants forever; His kingdom will never end (Luke 1:30–33).*

Gabriel spells it right out: for God has selected her to be the earthly parent of the Son of God. As we all would be, Mary is quite skeptical and replies, *How will this be … since I am a virgin? (Luke 1:34).*

In Gabriel's following response, he gives Mary a clue as to how she can prove that the request was authentic. Gabriel says, *The Holy Spirit will come on you, and the power of the Most High will overshadow you. So the Holy One to be born will be called the Son of God. Even Elizabeth your relative is going to have a child in her old age, and she who was said to be unable to conceive is in her sixth month. For no word from God will ever fail (Luke 1:35–37).*

When Mary heard the angel speak of her relative Elizabeth, she knew it must be real. Elizabeth, likely her aunt, had become pregnant at a very old age. She knew of this pregnancy and its remarkability. She had suspected this pregnancy was a gift from God, and now it was confirmed.

As a side note, Elizabeth, who was barren for many years, was pregnant with a son called John the Baptist. The same John who would later be the one in the wilderness who would proclaim Jesus as the *Lamb of God.* John would pave the way for Jesus.

Back to Mary, who prepared for a journey to visit Elizabeth—in a way, to confirm what Gabriel had told her. As Mary entered Elizabeth's house, the baby in her womb moved enthusiastically, and Elizabeth felt herself become filled with the Holy Spirit. Immediately she humbled herself and said, *But why am I so favored, that the Mother of my Lord should come to me?* (Luke 1:43)

Now Mary was convinced through this visit that what Gabriel had said was real, and she thankfully and humbly accepted this course in her life.

Immediately after, she said the words that are now famous and called

The Magnificat or Mary's Song:

My soul glorifies the Lord
  and my spirit rejoices in God my Savior,
for He has been mindful
  of the humble state of His servant.
From now on all generations will call me blessed,
  for the Mighty One has done great things for
  me—holy is His name.
His mercy extends to those who fear Him,
  from generation to generation.
He has performed mighty deeds with His arm;
  He has scattered those who are proud in their
  inmost thoughts.
He has brought down rulers from their thrones
  but has lifted up the humble.
He has filled the hungry with good things
  but has sent the rich away empty.
He has helped His servant Israel,
  remembering to be merciful

to Abraham and his descendants forever,
    just as He promised our ancestors.
(Luke 1:46–55)

This poem gives a few clues about why God picked Mary. The first is her humility; she didn't boast at the honor of being the mother of Jesus. She was humbled. Second, we can see from this poem her faith and knowledge.

Mary was far more than just an engaged teenager from a small town in Judea. She had faith, even though she knew there would be tongue clucking by her community. She knew that Joseph would be alarmed and suspicious. She also knew God would resolve all these negative aspects of her pregnancy.

Mary did deliver the Son of God. She was also a good mother. As a youth, she tended to Him, followed silently along through His ministry, and was there on the fateful day He died on a cross.

Like all who do big things for God, Mary is a model. While she had initial doubts, once she was sure it was God asking, she was all in. She was not boastful but humbled. What Mary did was very big! Mary's faith helped create a remarkable event for humankind: the arrival of the Son of God.

Mary and Tricia didn't have some self-created grand plan. Instead of thinking small, which would have been the safest route, they thought big. They knew they had help from God. To accomplish big things, we can't give in to doubt. Instead, follow faithfully the course of the river to the unknown, which Jesus has placed before us. For Jesus to be everything to us, we must follow faithfully and think *big*!

12

Give Up Control to Gain Jesus

*Take My yoke upon you and learn from Me, for I am
gentle and humble in heart, and you will find rest for
your souls.*

—Matthew 11:29

For Jesus to be our everything, we must
also give up control of our lives and turn our lives over to Jesus.
That is easy to say but far harder action to accomplish. Simply
saying *I will turn everything over to Jesus* is one of those promises
that has to be put into practice daily and with intensity.

We all start moving away from Jesus the moment we are
born. We learn how to get things through our own behavior.
What we see becomes a learning process on its own. Even the
sense of touch moves us away. We are training ourselves from
the very beginning on how to gain control of our lives. All this
needs to be undone to give up control and become born again.

We will even apply this sense of control to Jesus, making
Him in our minds what we want instead of what we need. Ironically, the better we are at gaining this illusionary sense of control, the more it pushes us further away from Jesus.

The simple truth is the more we give into Jesus, the more
freedom and control we gain. In Matthew 11:29, Jesus explains

this by saying, *Take My yoke upon you and learn from Me, for I am gentle and humble in heart, and you will find rest for your souls.* Giving up our control takes practice.

The Apostle Paul Lost Everything to Gain Jesus

Before accepting Jesus as Lord, Saul of Tarsus thought he was in complete control of his life. He had studied hard in his youth and became fluent in three languages. He knew scripture as well as any contemporary. At a young age, he was considered to be the Pharisee of the Pharisees. He was going to be a star. Everything he worked hard for was materializing for him. His life's path was sure and straight.

After Jesus had finished His ministry on earth, rose on the third day, and ascended to heaven, He left a growing and passionate group to carry on His mission. This bothered Saul, and to please his compatriots, the religious leaders in Jerusalem, he began to have these followers arrested and stoned.

Like most things in Saul's life, he approached this new path with zeal and a great deal of urgency. His goal was to eliminate these new troublesome followers of Jesus.

On one particular outing, he set off to Damascus to capture some of these followers. As he was traveling by horse, a light from heaven flashed around him. He fell from the horse and lay stunned on the ground. At this moment in his life, he became helpless and no longer in control of what was happening to him.

Jesus then said to him, *Saul, Saul, why do you persecute Me? Who are You, Lord?* Saul asked.

I am Jesus, whom you are persecuting, Jesus replied. *Now get up and go into the city, and you will be told what you must do.*

The other men traveling with Saul stood there speechless; they heard the sound but did not see anyone. Saul got up from the ground. When he opened his eyes, he could see nothing. He was blind and helpless. They led him by the hand into Damascus. For three days, he was blind and did not eat or drink anything (Acts 9:3–9).

Saul was no longer in control of anything. He was blind in a foreign city taken care of by total strangers. Everything he knew and controlled was now gone. He was an invalid without resources.

For three days, the same people he came to have arrested took care of him. On the third day, Jesus instructed one of these men, Ananias, to lay his hands on Saul's eyes, which he did. Immediately the scales, which had blinded him, fell away, and he was filled with the Holy Spirit. He got up, was baptized, and regained his strength. Those attending to him informed Saul it was Jesus who had met him on the way to Damascus.

When we go back to the events on the way to Damascus, we get an essential clue in this story. After Jesus asked Saul, *Why do you persecute Me?* Saul's answer was critical when he said, *Who are You, Lord?* Saul knew the divine was visiting him. He wasn't quite sure it was Jesus, but he knew it was his Lord. The beginning of his conversion started with the question, *Who are You, Lord?*

Now many of us know Saul as Paul. The same Paul would engage in three wonderful missionary trips throughout the Roman world, which helped make Christianity an international movement.

Some will say Jesus changed his name for effect. That is not true. Saul was Paul's Hebrew name, and Paul was his Roman name. After his conversion, Paul himself began using the name Paul.

At birth, he was both a Hebrew and a Roman citizen. Children born into these circumstances received two names: a Hebrew name, and a Latin name. In this case, Saul was his Hebrew name, and Paul was his Latin name.

Paul began using his Latin name exclusively, symbolic of the change made in him through his encounter with Jesus.

He would go on to become the great ambassador of Christianity. His early years as a new Christian were not easy. Many were suspicious of Paul and, at first, were dubious of his conversion. Paul himself was a little too exuberant and rubbed people the wrong way. For three years, Jesus sent him to Arabia to meditate on his experience and become a more chiseled follower.

Paul then spent time in Tarsus as a tentmaker until it was his time to help Jesus. This was a maturing time for Paul, an often missed period in his life, and a period of adjustment and cleansing of his need to control everything to allow him to become Jesus's great ambassador.

Paul had to lose everything to become a believer. His power and fame had to go, but so did his complete reliance on himself and very high need to control everything.

This is the same with us: To fully follow Jesus, we also have to let go. Some of the things we thought had made us successful have to be given up. We have to stand back and develop a strong faith in Jesus. It is our faith and taking Jesus's yoke that moves us forward.

Our Life's Mission Is Following Jesus

Brad went through a similar experience. He was having a successful business career. As time had moved on, he kept getting promoted and ended up in his company's highest echelon. Life had become easy for him; his bills were getting paid, and his savings were growing.

Over time, Brad had come to believe all the things he achieved were because of his hard work and uncompromising attitude. Those things in his life that were his dreams as a youth had become a reality. Everything was under control.

For the previous few years, Brad felt Jesus was asking him to let Him in. People would approach and ask him to serve in his church. He never seemed to have the time to answer any of these callings. There was always something more important to do. Simultaneously, he had begun to notice instinctively he would do the sign of the cross when something good happened.

At first, Brad was startled by this response. He even began to ask friends how to do the sign of the cross correctly. His minister would continue to ask him about getting more involved. Despite these events, he continued on his current path and would half-heartedly try to connect with Jesus.

After a few years passed, Brad was struck with a crisis in his life. All that he had worked for was now threatened. On a night when he couldn't sleep, he arose and began to walk the dark streets. As he walked searching for answers, he realized he had lost the ability to pray. A long-ago practice had disappeared. Sad and fearful, Brad could barely breathe.

As he continued to walk, he passed under a street light and noticed darkness behind him and light ahead. He stopped and asked Jesus to help. He tried a prayer, asking for help. What had been most important to him seemed lost. Undaunted now, he was committed to returning to Jesus, even if he had forgotten how to pray.

Later that day, he got a call from a close friend who told him he was worried about him. His friend began to talk about Jesus and how Jesus would help him. He also gave him a few verses to help him in his struggles.

That evening, he anxiously began to read the Bible, something he had long ago given up. As he was reading, he became overjoyed. He realized his prayers had been answered. Jesus had heard him. The friend who called and offered help was a sign Jesus had listened to his plea.

From this point, he began his long road back. One evening a few days later, and on another long evening walk, he sat on a bench and asked Jesus for help to rid himself of his selfishness. At that moment, he felt removed from his body. He began to watch a struggle for his soul. His selfishness would fight back time and time again, only to be met with the thoughts of only serving Jesus. For an hour, he watched this internal battle. This battle appeared to him to be a cosmic struggle. Finally, he said to himself, *I will only serve the Lord,* and left the bench.

Like Paul, the process of my friend's recovery was met with early zeal and excitement but was also uneven, and he stumbled often. The conversion to be what Jesus wanted him to be was uneven. There were many scales to be removed from his eyes from thinking he was in control of everything.

He never gave up and continued his journey. He recently told me about a time he was sitting on a step and realized his prayers had turned to helping others. At that moment, he knew he had made the turn. He realized that more and more of his thoughts were not about himself but of others' plights. He started to feel pain whenever he saw another person struggle. He no longer judged others but sought ways to comfort.

He gave up his time schedules and began to realize the Holy Spirit had organized things for him. This was a remarkable change for a person who in the past could carefully manage 100 items or more on a to-do list. He had taken Jesus's yoke and found it to be much lighter.

The more successful you have been on your own, the harder giving up control to Jesus is. Matthew 19:24 explains why successful people have a hard time with this concept by saying, *Again I tell you, it is easier for a camel to go through the eye of a needle than for someone who is rich to enter the Kingdom of God.* Essentially, these people became materially successful because they became good at exerting control. If our goal is to be materially successful, this might seem good, but it is a misguided path. If we understand our mission in life is following Jesus, we must relinquish control and follow Jesus.

Taking Jesus's Yoke

Not all control creates success. Sometimes the need to be in control is a result of trauma or predisposition. Controlling behavior is often associated with higher-than-normal anxiety levels. The person with over-controlling behavior has anxiety levels greater than their intellect and coping abilities.

Trauma or loss of control as a child will create this behavior in adulthood. The need for stability was disrupted and is now a sought-after desire. Statements like *I need this now* need to be replaced with *I feel anxious about this. How can we get this done together?* For the person with control issues, this would be a monumental leap.

The resolution of anxiety that creates control from a Christian perspective lies with Jesus, bringing us back to the verse from Matthew 11:29: *Take My yoke upon you and learn from Me, for I am gentle and humble in heart, and you will find rest for your souls,* believing this is the step that first must be taken. It is a matter of faith. Faith in Jesus is the first step, followed by taking Jesus's yoke.

This hurdle of giving up control and following Jesus has been a difficult step for many. It is a matter of faith. Faith, not in what you know but instead in who Jesus is—a choice we will all have to fulfill in our desire to make Jesus our everything.

Epilogue

Making Jesus a Full-Time Presence in Our Lives

So in Christ Jesus you are all children of God through faith.

—Galatians 3:26

The more you do anything, the more you want to do. Conversely, the less you do, the less you want to do. This thought seems ironic to me. Yet, it is as valid a statement as any that exists. And this concept applies to our relationship with Jesus as well. There is no middle ground here. We are either moving forward in our relationship with Jesus or moving further away.

I know a widow, Dorothy, who has been dealing with inertia in her life because of the death of her husband. She was stuck in a rut. Always a lifelong fitness pursuer, she found herself moving less and getting weaker. She was aging quickly and knew she had to get up and move.

She was energetic and vital for most of her life, always appearing and acting much younger than her age. Now, this seemed to be slipping away. She needed to get moving again. She began to start taking long walks. At first, two or three miles seemed long.

Resolutely, she kept walking despite her fatigue. Soon the half-mile hills were no longer challenging. She noticed that after a couple of weeks, four-mile walks were now her goal. Then in the next week, she started walking five miles and adding more hills. She began to walk on mountain trails and surprised herself with how far she could hike.

After a month, she tackled a walk almost six miles in length and gained 700 feet in elevation. To her amazement, she began to pass other hikers. She didn't need to stop as much to catch her breath. She began to feel vital and alive again.

At the age of eighty-seven, when many of her friends had stopped and fallen into poor health, she had regained her vitality.

One day after a powerful nor'easter had dumped a lot of snow, many people told her not to shovel. Recoiling at being told she was incapable of shoveling, she was determined to clear her driveway. She dressed and went out to get it done. Cautioned by knowing that shoveling can be dangerous if done too quickly, she slowly began to fill up her shovel with snow. Pacing herself, after 15 minutes, she noticed that she was making progress.

Neighbors came by and asked her if they could help. She thanked them but told the neighbors she was good. Slowly and without overdoing it, her driveway began to be cleared. She retired to the house and sat down with a great deal of joy. She did it!

Next, she tackled bringing up her Christmas tree from the basement. This would be the first time in 70 years that she put up her tree without her husband. Both sad and joyful, she put up the tree. She felt sad because her 70-year partner was missing the annual ritual, but she was joyful that she was moving again.

All of us could understand if she stayed on her couch. Aging and being without the person she had experienced 70 Christmases with, she certainly had a good excuse. A woman of faith, she knew she couldn't give in to depression or age. And she didn't want to quit just yet in life.

This story is also similar to our faith lives. Sure, there are times when we don't feel like praying, but when we are done, we are happier. The less we pray, the less we want to pray. The less we read the words of God, the less we desire the words of God.

This is the truth of life in all things. It is certainly true in our relationship with Jesus. The more we reach out and see a response, the more we want to reach out. The key is getting over the initial hurdle of rationalizing why we don't have time for Jesus. Once we do, we are on the road to a wonderful relationship with our King and Lord.

The thing about biblical habits is they take 40 days to cement. Around day 90, our lives change. This is the challenge we all must face. Are we capable of resisting the urge to stay lethargic or move on with our lives with Jesus?

Observing Jesus in Your Life

Another important aspect in our lives is becoming thoughtful observers of Jesus's responses. Seeing and understanding these responses requires careful and constant study. Know that Jesus will always respond. At first, our understanding of these responses may be limited. Know this: the more we observe, the more we will understand.

A former classmate, Wendy, gave me some helpful insight into how to watch for these responses. Wendy is a tall and powerful person in spirit. From her emanated a spirit that was strongly connected to Jesus. From our first conversation, I could tell most everything she thought and said was somehow related to Jesus. Her forthrightness was not phony or made up. She truly believed that all of her life was connected in some way to Jesus.

In one conversation, she asked of me, *Do you receive unusual and intimate responses from Jesus?*

After a brief moment of digesting this unusual question, I said, *I do. Why do you ask?*

Her reply: *I always do and want to make sure I am not alone in these experiences.*

At this point in my journey with Jesus, as a beginning theological student, a powerful statement like this also gave me confidence that I wasn't alone. As I talked with other classmates, not quite as bold as Wendy, I got similar responses. Later, when discussing this with other people of faith, I also observed that they experienced similar occurrences.

As Wendy and I talked, we tossed around questions. *Why were these responses unusual and not coincidental? And how did we know they were meant for us?*

After studying this for many years, I came to the following conclusions. First, Jesus knows better than us what we need. His wisdom is infinite, and ours is finite. When we go to Jesus, no matter how well-thought-out our request, Jesus's answers will always be better.

Secondly, Jesus is always trying to get our attention to ensure we know it is Him. I concluded that this is why the responses are so unusual and designed personally for us to know Jesus has heard us.

Sometimes we make requests for very specific items like healing, a positive outcome on an assignment, or a resolution to a problematic situation. The answer may come back as a change of perspective in what we want, perhaps a reorienting of why we want something, or maybe an unusual resolution to our request.

For some, this process is easy. But for most, observing and recognizing the answers take practice. Like any worthy effort, we need to be earnest and patient with ourselves.

I frequently find myself studying the response for an extended period before I act. Often, a particular item in my prayer or observation will come to mind, and I know it is the Holy Spirit helping me in my prayer.

When we look for a response, there are a few things we should know. Jesus will give us what we need and not what we want. This means we sometimes will be disappointed initially, only to understand later it was best. Jesus's answer will never be opposite to the will or Word of God. Jesus will never send us to a place where He won't provide the resources to succeed. Always know that Jesus loves you and is acting with your best interests at heart.

This observation time shouldn't be reacted to in haste; rather, it is a time of reflection and patience in letting events play out. The more complicated the answer, the longer we should let events unfurl.

When we sit and ponder what has happened, we should always test what we have seen with what we know is right. Jesus will never ask us to do or answer with something wrong. The more we wait and ponder, the clearer the picture will become. There may be many steps we have to take, and each one should be carefully measured. This period of reflection and waiting chisels us to be stronger and more faithful.

In this time of waiting, our mind becomes more accepting of Jesus's way. We soften our emotions and, in turn, accept the response, which in turn makes us more resolute. At some point, we will arise, firm in our convictions, and march forward. We will have confidence our course is set and no longer worry if we see things through murky eyes.

Be Blessed!

Making Jesus everything in our lives will not always be easy, yet it will always be worthwhile. In our climb up the mountain of faith, there will be times when we have to take slow and sure steps—never looking back, always looking ahead. Never be dismayed by how far you have to go, but be satisfied with the journey. Being close to Jesus is not just about the destination. The journey is just as important.

Today, reach out to touch Jesus and watch your life become more hopeful. Watch your life have meaning and certainty. Know this: Jesus is the only permanent part of our lives that we can always count on. Jesus isn't just what we need. Ultimately, Jesus is all we have.

Be blessed in your journey toward Jesus being everything to you.

www.ingramcontent.com/pod-product-compliance
Lightning Source LLC
LaVergne TN
LVHW041230080426
835508LV00011B/1140